THE PHENOMENON OF CHRISTIAN BELIEF

THE PHENOMENON OF CHRISTIAN BELIEF

Edited by

G. W. H. LAMPE

Ely Professor of Divinity, University of Cambridge

LONDON

A. R. MOWBRAY & CO LTD

Printed in Great Britain by
Alden & Mowbray Ltd
at the Alden Press, Oxford

SBN 264 64514 6

First published in 1970

ACKNOWLEDGEMENTS

The thanks of the author and publishers are due to the following for permission to quote extracts: Cambridge University Press, *The Natural and the Supernatural* by John Oman; T. & T. Clark, *Church Dogmatics* by Karl Barth; Eyre & Spottiswoode (Publishers) Ltd., *Riders in the Chariot* by Patrick White; Faber & Faber Ltd., *Collected Poems 1909 - 1962* and *Four Quartets* by T. S. Eliot, *About the House* and *Collected Shorter Poems 1927 - 1957* by W. H. Auden; Jonathan Cape Ltd., *Selected Poems* by C. Day Lewis; Prism Publications Ltd., *On Praying* by Alan Ecclestone; S.C.M. Press Ltd., *Word and Faith* by Gerhard Ebeling; S.P.C.K., an article in *Theology* by Lady Oppenheimer.

v

CONTENTS

EDITOR'S FOREWORD

For a number of years it has been the practice of the Board of the Faculty of Divinity at Cambridge to arrange an annual series of Open Lectures on matters directly or indirectly related to the problems of religious belief. These lectures are not part of the Faculty's regular course of theological teaching. They usually take place outside the Divinity School, and they are intended, not for specialists in religious studies of any kind, but for a general audience of people, mainly, but by no means exclusively, undergraduate, whose courses of study may lie in other fields, but who are interested in listening to a non-technical presentation of questions with which theologians are concerned and perhaps also in taking part in discussions which are arranged to follow the lectures. Such discussions cannot be reproduced in book form; but it is still to the general reader that these lectures, which are printed as they were delivered, are now addressed.

Some earlier courses of these Open Lectures have been devoted to particular questions of social and personal morality, such as the series on *God, Sex and War*[1] delivered in 1962. Others have discussed the basic problems of Christian belief itself and, especially in the crowded, and afterwards widely read, lectures on *Objections to Christian Belief*[2] in 1963, have adopted a rigorously critical attitude towards Christian doctrine. For the course in 1969 it was decided to

[1] Collins, Fontana Books, 1963.   [2] Constable.

attempt a more positive presentation of the belief of Christians. The object of these lectures is, as Mr Baelz points out at the beginning of his own contribution, to try to 'get clear in our minds what kind of thing Christian belief is and what kind of thing it is not'. The aim is to describe the phenomenon of Christian belief: not to undertake the task of an apologist and to contend for the truth of Christian belief, but to show what it is, at least in certain of its aspects.

It is, nevertheless, an attempt to describe this faith from the inside. The lecturers are trying to show how it appears to them, not as neutral observers, but as committed believers who in fact hold it to be true. They are speaking from within a living tradition which, because it is living and developing, is neither bound to a particular system of doctrinal orthodoxy nor compatible with static uniformity. Each lecturer is therefore attempting to describe Christian belief from his own individual standpoint, as he himself believes it. For the same reason, each looks back to the basic documents of Christian belief, the writings of the Old and New Testaments and the credal formulations of the early Church, from his own point of view and in a perspective conditioned by his personal belief. For the purpose of this descriptive task he is concerned, in the first instance, with the impact which these writings make on himself, and not primarily with the first aim of exegesis, which is the detailed analysis of the meaning and intention of the original writers; though this does not of course mean that his individual understanding and evaluation can dispense with scholarship.

The first lecture speaks of an 'adventure in exploration': 'the sort of thing it is for a Christian to believe in God and the way in which this belief is rooted in a living historical tradition'. The second looks back to the sources of that living tradition in the personal faith of Jesus himself as this is mirrored by the New Testament, and in the belief of his first followers that through Jesus God had made known to them his presence and power as 'the God and Father of our Lord Jesus Christ'. In the third lecture we are shown what Christians did with that original belief, why they constructed impressive but perplexing dogmatic formulations, and what relation these credal structures have to the faith by which the Christian community actually lives. The fourth enters into the heart of the life of Christian groups and individuals, and looks from the inside at the central activity which both expresses and stimulates Christian belief. It speaks of prayer from a personal and aesthetic standpoint.

The four lecturers were all at the time members of the Cambridge Faculty of Divinity.

The Rev. P. R. Baelz is the Dean of Jesus College and a lecturer in the Philosophy of Religion.

Canon G. W. H. Lampe is the Ely Professor of Divinity, with the New Testament and the Fathers as his fields of study.

The Rev. M. Santer is the Dean of Clare College, and a lecturer in Christian Doctrine.

The Rev. J. H. Drury was the Chaplain of Downing College when these lectures were delivered, and has since become Fellow and Chaplain of Exeter College, Oxford.

THE PHENOMENON OF CHRISTIAN BELIEF

THE KINGDOM OF GOD CHRISTIAN BELIEF

I

BELIEVING

BY

PETER BAELZ

THE TITLE of this series of four lectures has, I like to think, been chosen with due deliberation and care. It is not, you will have observed, the truth of Christian belief that is the immediate subject of discussion, but the phenomenon of Christian belief—Christian belief as it appears. This is not to suggest that the issue of truth is unimportant or that it is in no way our concern. On the contrary, it is, and must always be, the central issue confronting faith. Moreover I, for one, have no wish to circumvent this issue by transposing it into a different key and speaking with calculated ambiguity of the poetically true or the true-for-me. The true-for-me, which is not in principle also the true-for-you, to my mind lacks the fundamental constituent of truth altogether. Nevertheless, if we wish to do anything like justice to the questions of truth and falsity, we must first get clear in our minds what kind of thing Christian belief is and what kind of thing it is not. Only then shall we be in a position to judge whether or not it is true.

It would be possible to treat the phenomenon of Christian belief in a variety of ways, according to our different concerns. For example, social, cultural, or psychological treatments all have a validity within their own terms of reference. If you can establish that Christian belief is a bourgeois phenomenon, you have certainly established something. But do not run away with the idea that you have established everything. Even a bourgeois belief might, I suppose, be true! Our particular concern, however, is with the way that Christian belief appears to four reasonably ordinary people who find themselves, perhaps not altogether without an element of surprise, and certainly not without a persistent need to ask questions, confessing the Christian faith and seeking to understand the nature, ground and *raison d'être* of their belief.

The aim of these lectures, then, is descriptive rather than apologetic. We shall attempt to give some account of Christian belief as it appears to us from within the living Christian tradition. To speak 'from within' has its obvious dangers and disadvantages. It is all too easy, to say the least, to forget that there is also a 'without', and that to see ourselves as others see us is a grace for which we should all devoutly pray. On the other hand, the man who plays the game sometimes has a better grasp of its essentials than the man who merely observes. And if anyone is afraid that he is in for some kind of esoteric rigmarole, may I try to alleviate his fears by remarking that the lecturers are all children of the twentieth century as much as they are professing Christians, alive to the astounding advances of contemporary science and technology, alive also to the deep-seated moral and cultural scepticism which has developed side by side with an increasing moral passion and sensitivity. In such a situation as this it is inevitable that faith itself is born and lives under stress and strain. Whatever may be said about the assurance and certainties of faith, it is no stranger to perplexity and conflict. Its symbol could well be that of Jacob wrestling with God by the brook Jabbok through the night until daybreak: 'I will not let thee go, except thou bless me.' Contemporary faith knows that it must wrestle with God, man and the world, and in the wrestling seek a blessing.

One further word by way of preliminaries. We shall be concerned with the basic structure of Christian belief in God rather than with the development of theological systems. We are all old-fashioned enough to think that belief in God is a fundamental co-ordinate of Christian thinking, and it is this specific dimension of belief that we wish to explore. There are those, we know, who commend a sort of Christian atheism. That some of them sometimes have something important to say need not be denied. That the Christian idea of God (reputedly drawn after the pattern of the man who suffered under Pontius Pilate, was crucified, dead and buried) has all too often been recast in the shape of human dreams of power and glory is a fact of ecclesiastical history which it would be hypocritical to pretend were otherwise. If such is the all-too-human and tyrannical idea of God to which we really cling, whatever we may say to the contrary, then long may he be dead! But this particular hare we shall not be chasing. I introduce it for another reason. Although we shall all be attempting to describe how Christian belief appears to us from within the living tradition, the fact that the tradition is indeed living means that it is continually undergoing change and development. It follows that the detailed way in which Christian belief will appear to the believer may vary from age to age and even from person to person. Therefore in any description of the phenomenon of Christian belief, even when it comes from within the Christian tradition rather than from outside it, you must expect to find the believer's own understanding and evaluation involved. This need not make such a description arbitrary, or simply a matter of private opinion. There are canons and criteria of judgment, although it is no easy task to formulate them with precision. It is not the case that absolutely anything goes. But neither is it the case that we can be certain at any period of history just what goes. The contents of Christian theology are problematical rather than demonstrative, its pursuit tentative rather than deductive. The upshot of these somewhat apophthegmatic remarks, for which I ask your forbearance, is to remind you that no description of Christian belief can be made from a vantage-point of incontrovertibility. Therefore the views expressed by your four lecturers are inevitably their own personal views, though, one hopes, they are none the worse for being that. If they share a common mind, it is the conviction that the Christian tradition contains within itself both the demand and the resources for reformation and, if need be, for revolution.

In this lecture I want to attempt two things. First, I want to give an impressionistic account of the kind of thing that I take a Christian to be doing when he affirms his belief in God. And, second, I want to say something about the way in which such a belief arises and maintains itself. In the first instance, then, I shall, as it were, be stopping the film and examining a single frame, pointing to various of its details and suggesting their overall significance. In the second instance, I shall set the film moving again so that we can see the relation between this frame and those which have gone before and those which may come after. I speak of an 'impressionistic account' because I shall be selecting certain features of the still which seem to me of special interest and

importance, although I freely admit that there are many
other equally interesting and important things which might
be said and which on other occasions ought to be said.
Furthermore, I am conscious of the peculiar difficulty of
speaking about God at all. There are, I confess, times when
I wonder whether this difficulty is not simply due to the fact
that the whole notion of God is incoherent and nonsensical.
It would not be surprising if there were difficulty in speaking
sensibly and coherently about something which is nonsensical and incoherent.

> The other day upon the stair
> I met a man who was not there.
> I met him there again today:
> I wish the man would go away!

Is such nursery doggerel the true paradigm of what theologians sometimes call the splendid paradoxes of religion? On
the other hand, if God is, and if he is God, the supreme
object of worship and the One whose being and love always
exceed our limited understanding, so that we can be more
or less certain that at the very moment when we feel
tempted to exclaim that we have grasped God we are on the
point of losing him—after all it is a truism of Christian faith
that it is God who grasps us, and not we who grasp God—if
all this is in fact the case, then it is inevitable that our talk
about God should continually show signs of falling apart
and that silence should itself form a constitutive part of our
confession of faith. As Jacques Durandeaux, a French
philosopher–priest, has recently written: 'A man experiences
the necessity to speak and the necessity to keep silent. His
discourse leads him back to silence, and his silence is itself a

discourse which he must sooner or later explain. The paradox of the ineffable is that it is expressed and that if it were not expressed ineffability would not exist. By the same token the experience of God is the paradox of paradoxes—one finds it absolutely necessary to keep silent while experiencing an absolute necessity to speak.[1] To put it succinctly, if we do not keep silent about God, our speech loses its proper content; but if we do not speak about God, our silence loses its proper power. The words of T. S. Eliot in *East Coker* aptly convey the kind of thing that I should wish to say about the whole venture of talking about God:

> So here I am, in the middle way, having had twenty
> years—
> Twenty years largely wasted, the years of *l'entre deux
> guerres*—
> Trying to learn to use words, and every attempt
> Is a wholly new start, and a different kind of failure
> Because one has only learnt to get the better of words
> For the thing one no longer has to say, or the way in
> which
> One is no longer disposed to say it. And so each
> venture
> Is a new beginning, a raid on the inarticulate
> With shabby equipment always deteriorating
> In the general mess of imprecision of feeling,
> Undisciplined squads of emotion. And what there is to
> conquer
> By strength and submission, has already been dis-
> covered

[1] *Living Questions to Dead Gods*, Geoffrey Chapman.

Once or twice, or several times, by men whom one
    cannot hope
To emulate—but there is no competition—
There is only the fight to recover what has been lost
And found and lost again and again: and now, under
    conditions
That seem unpropitious. But perhaps neither gain nor
    loss.
For us, there is only the trying. The rest is not our
    business.[1]

Let us begin our raid on the inarticulate by asking ourselves *in what kind of context* an affirmation of belief in God is
at home. To what sort of questions could it be an 'answer'?
Certainly not to what we may call straightforward scientific
or historical questions. The frames of reference adopted by
the scientist or the historian in his professional capacity
leave no room for the introduction of the idea of God. There
is no need of that hypothesis. In so far as God can explain
anything and everything, he can explain nothing. For an
explanation to have any scientific or historical value it must
work within certain well-defined limits. To speak, then, of
the 'God-hypothesis' may be to use a misleading kind of
language, to put up the wrong frames of reference and to
suggest that we look for God-answers to questions where
such answers would be out of place.

The kinds of questions, I suggest, to which belief in God
may provide one possible response, are both highly general
and deeply personal. For example—What is the meaning of
life? Has life a meaning other than the meanings which you

---

[1] *The Complete Poems and Plays of T. S. Eliot*, Faber and Faber.

and I give to it, each of us in his own circumstances and with his own purposes and values? Again—Who am I? Where do I belong in this vast scheme of things? Basic questions, touching the foundations of our thinking and living. A Swiss theologian, Gerhard Ebeling, has pointed to this 'sphere of radical questionableness' as 'the condition on which it is possible for the problem of a natural knowledge of God to arise'. He writes: 'What the word "God" means can in the first instance according to its structure be described only as a question. The man who does not venture to ask questions is closed to the meaning of the word "God". To him the word "God" says absolutely nothing. The questionableness which encounters us along with the encountering reality provides, however vaguely, the reason why it can be claimed that what is said of God concerns every man and therefore can also in principle be intelligible to every man—*viz*. because it relates to something that has to do with the reality which encounters him.'[1] The radical questionableness which, I take it, the writer has in mind does not refer to the questionings which arise within any one chosen frame of reference, scientific, historical, moral, political and so on, which itself supplies the criteria for answering such questions, but to our frames of reference themselves. As human beings we respond to life by adopting various points of view for various purposes. Corresponding to the variety of our points of view is a variety of our horizons. Now we are chemists or physicists, now we are politicians, dons or undergraduates, now we are husbands, parents or children. At one time we are concerned with making a career, at another with making a home, at yet another with making

[1] *Word and Faith*, SCM, p. 347.

music or making love. We fashion webs of meaning around us, and life is such that it seems to support some and to reject others. Human life as a whole is a complex interlacing of such webs of meaning. But each web has a limited significance and constitutes a limited horizon. And sometimes they get across each other and become tangled, and at others they are broken either by circumstance or by our own clumsiness. What, if anything, lies beyond our limited horizons? What, if anything, undergirds our persistent, human quest for meaning and prompts our search for a truly personal and integrated humanity?

These are questions, as I have suggested, at once of a highly general and a deeply personal nature. They concern life as a whole, in all its many aspects of weal and woe, chance and destiny, success and failure, triumph and tragedy, agony and glory, hope and despair. They concern not this or that particular experience, but all experience, past, present and future. They raise the question of a vantage-point beyond all vantage-points—a question which, once uttered, threatens to lapse into meaninglessness, but nevertheless a question which refuses to be exorcised and silenced.

Now, general and all-embracing as these questions are, they are not remote or abstract. They rise for us as at the personal level, that is, as we try to discover our own true humanity and penetrate to deeper levels of self-knowledge. They concern the ways in which we see ourselves and make ourselves and our worlds in the drama of life. They call for decision and action as well as for reflection. They are 'existential' questions, not simply theoretical questions. It has been recently suggested that a key to human action and feeling is to be found, not simply in the will to be, but more specifically in the will to belong. We may, then, express the personal aspect of our radical questioning in the form: where do I really belong?

Man's search for where he really belongs produces a number of different answers. I have a past, by which I have been shaped. If I look to my past I may say that I belong to nature, or to my race, or to the culture in which I have been born and bred. In a perfectly proper sense I belong to all of these. I can trace my heritage through my cultural and racial ancestry, and thence further back through my animal ancestry, and still further back along the whole course of evolution—living, organic and inorganic. I can understand to a greater or lesser extent the processes which have gone into my making and led to my being what I am. But I have a future as well as a past; and if I look to the future I may say that I belong to humanity, to a future that awaits my own shaping in conjunction with the creative activity of others. Between my past and my future lies my present, my sphere of personal responsibility. In the light of this I may say that I belong to myself, that I am free to choose myself and my world according to my own self-imposed purposes. All these points of view contain a measure of truth. This is hardly open to dispute. But how are they to be related to one another? Is there any continuity of meaning to be discerned in my history, my destiny and my freedom? Is any of these points of view more fundamental, more comprehensive, than the others? Am I at heart a naturalist or a racialist, a humanist or an existentialist? Is there any unity of being to be discovered and achieved, or must I rest content with a plurality of viewpoints and horizons, one to be substituted for another like different clothes for different occasions? And if this latter is the case, can I achieve any personal integrity throughout such a chameleon-like existence? Is there any unity of my being, behind the many masks I wear?

Now, belief in God is the conviction that I really belong to God, and that my heart will be restless until it finds its rest in him. This is not to deny that I belong in an important sense to nature, humanity or myself. It is not even to set up *another* home where I belong, alongside of and separate from nature, humanity and myself. To do this would be to suggest that I do not in any important sense belong to nature, humanity and myself. It would constitute a kind of closed shop, an idolatry of religion. The first function of the affirmation that I belong to God is to combat all idolatries, including religious idolatry, to oppose my innate tendency to erect a false absolute out of that which is essentially relative, and to place a 'No Thoroughfare' sign against the roads which turn nature into Nature, humanity into Humanity and myself into Myself. That God can liberate me from my idolatries is, indeed, one of the ways in which I may become aware of his gracious presence. Consider the following reflections: 'How can we ever identify the presence of grace, since notoriously there can be nothing to contrast it with? I should like to suggest, certainly not a solution, but a slight abatement of the problem. There is a situation which one can at least begin to contrast with the presence of God: not His absence, but the presence of a false God. One sometimes becomes aware that one has been making God in one's own image and praying habitually to an idol, an idol who can even be made to give answers but whose answers will always be the perpetual reflections of one's own thoughts. The unwelcome character of some of these answers does not ensure their objectivity: one can insult oneself, harangue oneself, blame oneself, deny oneself, and still hear no voice but one's own. To reject this idol may often involve falling back upon scepticism, but sometimes one seems fleetingly to be enabled to reject the idol in the name of a Being who really is Another, who requires one to stop putting words into His mouth, who has the unpredictable disconcerting quality of the God of the New Testament, who directs one's attention away from oneself, who is relaxed where the idol is grim and immensely awe-inspiring where the idol is puny. There is no trick for getting in touch with this God, but just occasionally, and not at all according to merit, it seems as if a barrier had been removed. Who is to say He is not another idol? At least He is a more subtle and convincing one.'[1] I think I am on this writer's wavelength. I believe that there is in fact a liberation, a loosening up, in Christian faith and experience. This sense of liberation is, for the believer, a coming to himself and a coming to God—or, rather, a coming *of* God. It is both at the same time. It is a sense of ultimate and utter dependence on God, because God simply is the ultimate Being. He is, and there is nothing that you can do to make it otherwise! Nevertheless, the recognition of this fact, so far from detracting from man's freedom and responsibility, actually enhances and fulfils it. Thus the name of this God is not naked Power. It is Love, and in his service is man's perfect freedom. It is of this freedom-in-dependence that Paul speaks when he writes: 'All things are yours; whether Paul,

[1] Lady Helen Oppenheimer, in *Theology* Vol. 68, February, 1965, pp. 75 ff.

or Apollos, or Cephas, or the world, or life, or death, or
things present, or things to come; all are yours; and you are
Christ's; and Christ is God's!' What greater tribute to the
glory of man and his coming of age could we ask for than
that?

A remarkable and memorable expression of this union of
the all-embracing and yet personal constituents of Christian
belief in God has been given by the late Karl Barth, who,
whatever else may be said about him, knew better than most
what sort of talk it was to talk about God: 'He [the Christian]
sees what the others do not see. The world-process in which
he participates in solidarity with all other creatures might
just as easily be a vain thrusting and tumult without either
master or purpose. This is how many see it. But the Christian
sees in it a universal lordship. The lordship might just as
easily be that of natural law, or fate, or chance, or even the
devil. That is how many see it. But the Christian sees in it
the universal lordship of God, of the God who is the Father,
who is the Father to him, his Father. . . . If the relation
between the Creator and the creature is the relation which he
can see in Jesus Christ, then existence in this relation is the
existence which is to be truly desired, an existence in the
highest possible freedom and felicity. To have to confess
this is not an obscure law, but a friendly permission and
invitation. It is not unwillingly but spontaneously, not
grudgingly but gladly, that the Christian will affirm and lay
hold of this relation and his own existence in it. Hence the
reality does not cost him anything. He does not have to
force it. He does not have to struggle to attain it. It comes
to him in the same way as what he sees comes to him. And
this means that he does not screw himself up to a height

when he is a real creature. It also means that there does not arise any claim or merit on his part just because he confesses so unreservedly what other creatures and other men cannot and will not confess. The fact that he does so is not a kind of triumph for his individual honesty. Other people are just as honest, perhaps more so. He is simply made real by what he sees. And as such he is simply availing himself of a permission and invitation. He is going through an open door, but one which he himself has not opened, into a banqueting hall. And there he willingly takes his place under the table, in the company of publicans, in the company of beasts and plants and stones, accepting solidarity with them, being present simply as they are, as a creature of God. It is the fact that he sees, and that which he is able to see as the centre and the circumference, the Creator and the creature, which constitute the permission and invitation and open door to his peculiar reality.'[1] I hope you will accept this lengthy quotation both for its intrinsic value and as a tiny tribute to the man who has so far been the outstanding Christian theologian of the present century.

Let me now sum up what I have been trying to say so far. Belief in God is to be understood as a confession of faith. As such it possesses a double character. On the one hand it is a fundamental self-orientation. The believer adopts a stance from which he views all experience, and in the light of which he makes his response to every occurrence. It is his basic attitude to life, his ultimate concern—his faith, his hope, his love. If you like the expression, you can say that it is his all-inclusive commitment. On the other hand, and no less important, it is an affirmation that such a basic attitude

[1] *Church Dogmatics*, III, 3, T. & T. Clark, pp. 240 ff.

is not simply one that he himself happens to fancy or to find psychologically inviting, not simply true-for-himself because it happens to turn him on, but one which is the appropriate and proper response to experience and so the true response *tout court*. It is the character of reality as such which justifies this response. It is the fact *that God is* and *that God is Love* that makes this response the appropriate one. Thus the confession of faith involves a claim to cognition at the same time as the adoption of an attitude. It involves both belief and commitment; and although these cannot be divorced from one another, it is clear that the belief is logically prior to the commitment. The claim of faith is that the being of God is prior to the being of man, that God is Creator and man is creature. The commitment is seen as a response, the decision of faith as the recognition of grace. Whatever truth there may be in the assertion that man makes God in his own image, the affirmation of faith carries with it a clear distinction between the concept of God (which indeed is man-made, just as all human concepts are man-made) and God himself. Indeed, faith is especially sensitive to the dangers of anthropomorphism, to the temptation to see God as some enlarged and exalted version of Superman, even though the least inadequate way of talking about God may well be in terms of man's—more specifically, of Christ's— own personal being. Agnosticism is in many ways to be preferred to anthropomorphism, silence to speech. The incomprehensibility of God is an intrinsic part of the believer's understanding of God. Even to faith, in fact especially to faith, God remains fundamentally mysterious. Theology begins and ends in silence—the silence which is not emptiness, but the silence which is worship. When the believer confesses his faith in God and affirms that he belongs to God, he affirms that this mysterious God is also the one who gives final significance to nature and to history, the one who gives meaning to the human search for meanings, the one who is the explanation of the fact that there are explanations. He is the Beyond in our midst, the Light by which we see light.

Thus belief in God is not reached at the conclusion of an argument, whether demonstrative or merely probable, conducted within an agreed frame of reference which makes no mention of God. It is rather the appearance of a new and all-embracing frame of reference, the admission of a further and fundamental co-ordinate for mapping our experience. Belief in God introduces a way of seeing and interpreting man and nature in the light of that which transcends man and nature. The Christian believer affirms that all things at all times are to be seen for what they ultimately and truly are when they are seen within the context of the light of the divine creative and redemptive Love. Certainly, in so far as he confesses his faith in God he is committed to a belief in the One who may properly be called supernatural and superhistorical—for God is not to be located in the spheres of what, by the use of certain limited and limiting frames of reference, we call nature and history—but such a belief does not relegate God to some alien sphere of splendid isolation and inaccessibility. As eternal Light he is the light of the world. Beyond the world He is the Reality of the world. John Oman ended his masterly book on *The Natural and the Supernatural* with these words: 'If we would have any content in the eternal, it is from dealing whole-heartedly with the evanescent; if we would have any content in freedom it is by victory both without and within over the necessary; if we would have any content in mind and spirit we must know aright by valuing aright. If so, religion must be a large experience in which we grow in knowledge as we grow in humility and courage, in which we deal with life and not abstractions, and with God as the environment in which we live and move and have our being and not as an ecclesiastical formula. . . . Denying the world does not mean that we do not possess it in courageous use of all possibilities, but only that we do not allow it to possess us.'[1] To let the world possess us is what I think the Christian means when he talks about sin. To be freed from the power of sin is to come to see the world as it really is, with all its glory and tragedy, all its potential and limitations—that is, to see it in and under God.

If belief involves this kind of seeing, this kind of interpreting and reorientation, then we can more readily appreciate why the believer is accustomed to use the imagery of illumination and the still more violent imagery of rebirth, of death and resurrection. We can understand why the Psalmist prays: 'Open thou mine eyes that I may see the wondrous things of thy law'; why the Christ of the Fourth Gospel asserts: 'Except a man be born anew he cannot see the kingdom of God'; and why Paul writes to the Christians at Rome: 'Even so reckon ye also yourselves to be dead unto sin, but alive unto God in Christ Jesus.' These images are not in the first instance images of the moral life, although undoubtedly they are rich enough to have untold implications for the moral history of the believer. They are fundamentally images of the way of coming to believe in God.

[1] *The Natural and the Supernatural*, CUP.

C

Belief in God is a happening—in Barth's words, a permission and invitation. In theological parlance, faith is a gift of God himself. No doubt in certain contexts and for certain purposes it is right to talk of the 'decision' of faith. There has to be an acceptance of the gift, a response to that which shows itself to us. But faith is never a decision *in vacuo*, a leap in the dark. Keep the word 'leap' if you wish, for it does stress the novelty and discontinuity of faith; but let us talk, equally symbolically, but with an apter symbolism, of a leap into the light. To speak of a leap into the light suggests that there are continuities of faith with the other ways in which we know the world around us, that it is this same world, which we already know in part, which is now seen for what it truly and ultimately is by reason of the light which is eternal.

I have spoken of belief as a way of seeing, and I myself find this a helpful analogy. But at once I recognize the need to qualify such a way of speaking. Faith is traditionally contrasted with sight. Something like sight is reserved for the last day, when we shall know as we are now known and see God face to face. But now we see through a glass, darkly. Faith is a glimpsing rather than a full seeing. Man lives *in via* and not *in patria*, he is on the way, he has not arrived. The world, too, is in the making, imperfect and incomplete. It is precisely because of this fact that faith is often a wrestling and an agonising. It is open to sceptical attacks of doubt both at the personal and at the general level. Do I really glimpse what I believe I have glimpsed, or do I delude myself?

When I reflect on the infinite pains to which the human mind and heart will go in order to protect itself from the full impact of reality, when I recall the mordant analyses of religious belief which stem from the works of Karl Marx and Sigmund Freud and, furthermore, recognise the truth of so much of what these critics of religion have had to say, when I engage in a philosophical critique of the language of theology and am constrained to admit that it is a continual attempt to say what cannot properly be said and am thereby led to wonder whether its claim to cognition can possibly be valid—when I ask these questions of myself and others like them (as I cannot help asking and, what is more, feel obliged to ask), is not the conclusion forced upon me that my faith is a delusion? Can I still dare to believe in God?

I hope you will not expect any neat and satisfying answer to these difficult questions. They are too serious and searching to be disposed of by any quick retort. Nor do I think that they can be once and for all answered and set aside. They are the inescapable correlates of faith. In fact, I would go further, and say that faith itself demands that they should be taken seriously. Because faith can so easily degenerate into superstition and self-deception, it calls upon scepticism as its ally in its unceasing attempt to purify itself from superstitious and deceptive elements. I think I would say that one of the reasons why I am prepared to take faith seriously is because I find that faith takes scepticism seriously. Faith is not impervious to questions of integrity and truth. It reveals a passionate concern with both; but it realises that they are not neatly circumscribed nor easily achieved. Christian faith is built on the twin pillars of truth and love. Truth will not reveal its fullness except to a patient and persistent love; while a love which neglects the claims of truth degenerates into a sentimental and sometimes selfish affection.

Doubts arise both at the subjective and at the objective ends of belief. Take the subjective end first. Take any claim, however circumspect, to have some sense of the presence of God. Is it not all too likely to be a species of self-delusion? Is there anything about it which suggests that it may not be such? Part of what I should want to say in the face of this persistent and nagging question would run like this. In those all too rare moments when I seem to be aware of the gracious presence of God, the light which this sheds on myself gives me the strong conviction that now I recognise myself as I truly am in my innermost being. When I acknowledge myself as the creature of God, it is as if I were coming home after a journey into a far country. Furthermore, it is as if I were being drawn out of myself through a kind of self-forgetfulness into a concern with all that is real around me, a concern not only with God but with his whole creation. This experience is by no means always welcome, and certainly not immediately comforting. But then reality is not what we should always like it to be, and love is not always the sweet delight which the romantics like to paint it. All I can say is that this experience has the bite of reality. But how can I be sure that it is the real thing? I cannot, if in order to be sure I must establish some purely external system of proof. There can be no such decisive proof if believing in God is the kind of seeing and interpreting which I have suggested. In the last resort, the proof of the pudding is in the eating. And that is the irony of it all. But this, of itself, does not prove that I am mistaken. Take an analogy, rough and ready though it is. When I fall in love with the girl whom I propose to ask to be my wife, how do I know it is the real thing and not just one more of that extended series of infatuations that has marked my autobiography? There is no system of external tests which will put the matter once and for all beyond the range of doubt. But when I compare my present love for this girl with my previous loves for other girls, in comparison with them it has the bite of reality. It has a concern for her well-being at least as much as, perhaps more than, for my own, a desire to break through my own images and idealisations of the girl, my illusions about her, and at all costs to know her as she really is. I cannot prove to you that this is the real thing, but I am not being merely arbitrary and blind in believing that it is. I may be mistaken, but I shall continue to believe that I am right until I can be shown the error of my ways. I claim to have reason to believe, and this claim is not obviously a fraud.

I venture to speak in this way because I think that the logic of faith itself requires that some account be given of what Pascal has called the reasons of the heart. Nevertheless, this cannot be the whole story. Faith has an objective as well as a subjective side. There is a content to Christian belief; and this content too is open to criticism and subject to the sceptic's attack.

Belief in God claims to illuminate all experience. But does it? Does the belief that the whole world of nature and history is the creative and redemptive venture of eternal Love make sense? Does it cohere with what we know from other sources of man and the world in which he lives? Does it in fact illuminate, or does it render darkness darker still? The light of God, it may be said, is an odd sort of light, for it fails to illuminate. On the contrary, it puts the blinkers on!

It is one of the continuing tasks of theology to develop its beliefs in relation to the knowledge that we obtain from our empirical disciplines. These provide us with the material to be illuminated. As our empirical knowledge changes and develops, so the material that calls for illumination through belief in God changes and develops. Thus a living theology must change and develop. It is never final or complete. The attempt to think theologically in this way is the intellectual task which awaits the Christian believer. For example, how do we see the creative and redemptive love of God through the perspective of the age-long development of the immense universe, only a speck of which we inhabit, and of the evolution of sentient and rational life on this earth through thousands and millions of years? Can we speak of God and of his Love in such a way that it does justice to our increasing knowledge and power?

I said that this was the believer's theological task. And so it is. But I should be seriously misleading you if I were to give the impression that any theologian has satisfactorily completed this task for this day and age. I doubt whether it is a task which can ever be satisfactorily completed. On the other hand I do not consider the task hopeless. The attempts of such seers as Teilhard de Chardin to set the whole story of evolution in the light of the continually creative love of God have, I believe, despite their obvious deficiencies, much to offer us. But darkness remains, areas of darkness which seem to resist the power of such illumination. I refer especially to the whole mystery of evil. There is an element of the sheerly destructive, even of the demonic, in the world which is hard to square with belief in a God who is Love. It is this mystery of evil above all else which causes faith to tremble and to pray, 'Lead us not into temptation, but deliver us from evil.' In his great commentary on the Fourth Gospel Archbishop Temple commented on the words in the Prologue, 'and the light shineth in the darkness, and the darkness did not absorb it', as follows: 'Imagine yourself standing alone on some headland in a dark night. At the foot of the headland is a lighthouse or beacon, not casting rays on every side, but throwing one bar of light through the darkness. It is some such image that St John had before his mind. The divine light shines through the darkness of the world, cleaving it, but neither dispelling it nor quenched by it. . . . The darkness in no sense at all received the light; yet the light shone still undimmed. So strange is the relation of the light of God's revelation to the world which exists to be the medium of that revelation.'[1] The world is radically questionable. For the Christian believer it reflects more of the divine possibility than the divine accomplishment. He looks to the future, not simply to the past. If he believes that God is at the beginning as well as at the end, the Alpha as well as the Omega; if his hope for the future arises out of his faith in God's eternal presence; it is because he discerns the manner of God's presence and the way of his working in the strange person of Jesus of Nazareth, in his life and teaching, and not least in the bitter and apparently senseless tragedy of his death. Doubt continues to assail him from all sides, but belief in God mediated through the person of Jesus Christ is oddly persistent, and even the absence of God comes to echo his presence.

This brings me to the second and final part of this lecture. I have spoken at some length, though very inadequately, on the sort of thing that belief in God appears to me to be. You

[1] *Readings in St John's Gospel*, Macmillan.

may think that I have fallen between two stools, doing justice neither to the assurance of faith nor to the logical difficulties inherent in the content of belief. Be that as it may, in the last part of this lecture I wish to set the film moving again and to say something about how this faith arises and how it maintains itself. I have, of course, all along been referring, either implicitly or explicitly, to Christian belief, although I have been concerned more with its form than with its content. But the two cannot finally be kept apart, for Christian belief receives its peculiar stamp and structure from that living tradition in which Jesus Christ is acknowledged to be the defining centre. It is to this tradition that we shall now turn.

Christian belief in God arises out of and maintains itself within a specific historical tradition. Simply to say this, however, is not to say anything very startling. In a sense all our knowledge arises out of and maintains itself within a living tradition. Man is an historical being. He is shaped by his cultural and intellectual heritage however much he may rebel against it. The traditions of a community are techniques by which one generation hands on to the next the store of experience and knowledge which it has acquired. Mixed up with the gold there may be a lot of dross; but it is futile to imagine that each generation and each individual must start again from scratch in order to acquire a proper understanding of the world around them. The scientist as much as anyone else is dependent on the tradition of the scientific community, on its especial authority, responsibility and methods of going about its scientific tasks. It is not easy to pin-point what constitutes the scientific endeavour as such, but that there is a unity and continuity which holds together the whole developing scientific exploration I think there can be little doubt.

There is, however, a further sense in which Christian faith depends on a continuing historical tradition. Not only has it been forged and fashioned within a particular segment of human history, namely, Judaeo-Christian history, through which we can trace a development in the understanding of God and his relation to man and the world; but within this history certain happenings have been given a key place and the interpretation of these has been allowed to exercise a control over the ensuing development. Thus for the Jew the events of the Exodus and its interpretation as a covenant between God and Israel were given a constitutive function in the development and understanding of Jewish faith. They acted as a kind of norm, allowing some developments of belief, checking others. For the Christian this same constitutive function is exercised by the teaching, life and death of Jesus Christ, and by the affirmations about Jesus made by his disciples as a result of their Easter experiences. As the writer of the Letter to the Hebrews puts it: Jesus 'is the author and perfecter of faith', or, as the New English Bible has it, on him 'faith depends from start to finish'. He is not only the source of faith; he is also the object of faith. That is, in Jesus the Christian claims to see the divine love bodied forth, and his belief about God is controlled by his belief about Jesus.

To repeat, Christian belief in God has the teaching, work and person of Jesus Christ as its supreme norm. What sort of norm this is, what we can know about this norm, and how this norm is to be used are matters of hot contemporary theological controversy. Clearly there is no easy answer to these questions, and some may be tempted to abandon altogether the notion that Jesus Christ is the norm of Christian belief. The originator of a new and continually developing Christian tradition, yes; but the persistent norm, how can that be? How can anyone of the first century provide a norm for men of the twentieth century, let alone for men of the unnumbered centuries which we hope may follow after ours? The answer that we shall give to this question will depend on what it is that we are looking for. If it is some complete system of religious belief and practice, we shall certainly be disappointed. There is no such system to be found. If, however, it is a way of life, based on certain fundamental convictions concerning God, man and the world, and expressing a recognizable set of aims, objectives and approach, that is another matter. Just as we may argue that there is a unity of aims, objectives and approach underlying and generating empirical science, however greatly scientific beliefs may change and develop from age to age, so we may argue that there is an analogous unity underlying and generating Christian belief and practice. This unity originates from Jesus. *He* points the way: *we* have to make the journey. Jesus continues to communicate to men of different ages and different outlooks the belief in God which was his. Thus it is not a ready-made theological or ethical system which is the norm. It is rather a fundamental frame of reference for thinking and living, by which theologies and moralities may be developed in the light of growing and changing experience. It is, if you like, a person.

If Jesus is the norm of Christian belief, its principle and pattern, experience provides the content. The norm has continually to be expressed and embodied afresh in terms of contemporary experience. The Christian claim is that the light of God in Jesus illuminates all experience. Christian thinking and living must put this claim to the test. We may, then, almost speak of a double norm—though the norms function in rather different ways. An American theologian, Gordon Kaufman, has recently written: 'It is with reference to the historical norm that we can adjudge whether a given position or claim is "Christian"; it is with reference to the experiential norm that we adjudge whether it "makes sense".'[1] The plea that Christian faith should make sense and be shown to be relevant—blessed word!—both to life and thought is in fact a very proper plea, if for no other reason than that it claims for itself such relevance; but to establish some concept of 'relevance' as the criterion of Christian belief is a sad mistake. There is more than one way of 'being with it', and the way to truth and salvation is notoriously narrow!

A living tradition is one that possesses within itself the resources for its own self-criticism and renewal. In this sense tradition must be distinguished from traditions. Traditions are those specific forms of thought in which in each age the tradition embodies itself. They are also the means by which the tradition is handed down from one age to another. Although they may carry the living tradition, they also contain what is relative to a particular age. Traditions, therefore, have always to be reappraised and reassessed. To live from within a tradition is not the same thing as to be a traditionalist. In the process of handing on the tradition, of being faithful to the tradition, traditions have an essential part to play. Each age is dependent on the traditions of the community if it wishes to enter into the tradition. But if the

[1] *Systematic Theology: A Historicist Perspective*, Charles Scribners.

tradition is to continue to live, then each age and each individual must bring his own experience into the community, must make the tradition his own. And in the name of the tradition it may well be that certain traditions have to go. It does not seem to me absurd—although it is not a position to which I find myself compelled—that in the name of Christ a man should feel in conscience bound to reject the present institutional Church. That is, out of the living tradition he rejects the form in which the tradition has become embodied. In the name of the tradition he rejects the traditions. On the other hand, an indiscriminate repudiation of the traditions is incompatible with fidelity to the tradition. The traditions are not all of a piece. Some have a better claim to express and reflect the living tradition than others. Some die for one generation but come to life again for another. The relation between tradition and traditions, between the life of faith and the formulations and expressions of faith, is a highly complex one. Although we are bound to distinguish between them, in order to escape the dangers of a dying traditionalism, we may not wrench them asunder under the banner of a reckless radicalism. For the Christian, true radicalism lives out of the tradition itself. As Bishop Robinson expressed it in a sermon in Great St Mary's: 'It is Jesus Christ that gave me the roots to be a radical.' And whence do we learn of Jesus Christ except through the traditions in Bible and Church which proclaim him?

If Christian faith in God is not simply a natural faith, nor simply a rational belief, but derives from and depends upon a particular historical tradition, can it really be claimed that such belief is universally true? Surely truth ought in principle to be equally available to all men everywhere, especially truth about the ultimate Reality whom we call God? And if this is not the case, are there not other religious traditions, each with its own historical concept of the ultimately real, and their claims to truth?

These are searching questions. All that I have time to do now is to make two simple points. First, the affirmations which the Christian makes about God arise out of relationships which have been constituted and reconstituted between man and God, and history rather than nature or thought is the context in which such relation-making can occur. Furthermore, while affirming that the definitive relation between God and man has been accomplished in Jesus Christ, in one man in one place and at one time, the Christian goes on to affirm that into such a relationship all men are to be brought. Christian faith is universal in intent. It speaks of a relationship between God and man that in principle holds good for all men. But the principle is not a natural or a rational principle, nor a principle to be discovered at the beginning of history or throughout history. It is a principle to be realised in the future, what theologians call an eschatological principle. Realised once in Jesus Christ, it has yet to be realised for all. God is He who comes, not simply He who is. Second, to affirm that Jesus Christ is the norm of true belief in God is indeed to make what looks like a presumptuous and exclusive claim. And Christian history has been all too marred by presumption and exclusiveness. But to make this claim does not, as I see it, involve us in denying that there is much to be learned from other religious traditions, much which they can contribute to our understanding of the ways of God *and* to the correction of our misunderstanding of the ways of God. As the traditions engage with each other in dialogue, I envisage enrichment as well as conflict. What the claim does seem to me to involve is that the God of the future, the God of all humanity, will be discovered to be none other than the One whom Christians call the Father of Jesus Christ. To make even such a claim will seem to many to be parochial, to say the least. But put beside it the thought of the writer of the Fourth Gospel, that the Light which came into the world with Jesus was the light which enlightens every man.

I have tried to say something about the sort of thing it is for a Christian to believe in God and about the way in which this belief is rooted in a living historical tradition. I fear that my shabby equipment and general mess of imprecision may have made it all sound drear and dead. But in fact is does not feel like that at all. It is essentially an adventure in exploration, an exploration from God into God, and this ordinary, this extra-ordinary world in which we live is the place where the exploring must begin.

> We must be still and still moving
> Into another intensity
> For a further union, a deeper communion
> Through the dark cold and the empty desolation,
> The wave cry, the wind cry, the vast waters
> Of the petrel and the porpoise. In my end is my
>   beginning.[1]

Belief in God is not the end but the beginning of exploration.

[1] T. S. Eliot, *East Coker*.

2

THE GOD OF JESUS
BY
MARK SANTER

CHRISTIAN BELIEF is a traditional belief. When we say this, we mean more than just that it is old. We mean that if our beliefs are to qualify as Christian at all, they must inescapably be referred to tradition, to the beliefs of past Christians.

Now if we look at this tradition, at the beliefs of past Christians, we find that they in their turn have always felt bound to refer *their* beliefs to one particular piece of the tradition and to one particular generation of past believers— the generation of the apostles. Christians of all subsequent generations have always tried—even if one may think that they have not always succeeded—to treat the beliefs of that first generation as somehow normative for subsequent beliefs.

This belief in the primacy of that first generation and its beliefs takes a number of forms. One of them is the doctrine of the authoritative character of the particular writings which we call the New Testament. The reason why these books are authoritative is that they are the precipitate of the beliefs of those first believers. Writings, however edifying, which were not believed to have their origin in that first generation were deliberately excluded from Scripture, because they lacked this apostolic authority. Another form which belief in the primacy of that first generation has taken is the notion that revelation ceased with the death of the last apostle. Testimony is paid to this belief both by classical Roman Catholic theology, when it tries to show that the apostles knew all about the Bodily Assumption into heaven of the Blessed Virgin Mary, and also by new-fangled theologians when they try to claim Jesus as the first Christian atheist. There is a deep conviction in the Christian consciousness that beliefs which have since been formulated can be accepted as authoritative only if they can reasonably be seen as an explication of the known beliefs of Jesus and the apostles. If this were not so, there would never have been such a fuss about the work of New Testament criticism.

But is that really the point at which the story begins? Is the New Testament really the only fountainhead of our faith? Many people clearly think so. Their belief is expressed and encouraged by the way New Testaments are printed on their own as if they were all the Bible that one really needs. Again, liturgical practice encourages this belief: many of us hardly hear anything read in Church except the Scriptures of the New Testament. It is the New Testament which, for all practical purposes, actually functions as our Bible. Christianity is regarded as beginning with Christ. He is the so-called Founder of Christianity.

But if we look at the beliefs of Jesus and the apostles as they are mirrored in the New Testament, we find that they see themselves as standing not so much at the beginning as at the culmination of a tradition of faith. Just as subsequent generations of Christians inescapably refer themselves to Jesus and the apostles, so too Jesus and the apostles refer themselves to the beliefs of old Israel and to their precipitate in what we now call the Old Testament. For them *these* writings are Scripture, authoritative documents of their own faith. We see Jesus and his apostles as our ancestors in faith;

they saw Abraham and Moses as theirs. For all the discontinuity between the two testaments, there is immeasurably more continuity. There is a continuity of faith, which believes itself to be grounded in the continuity of the One who is believed in. That is the heart of the matter: the belief of the apostles, who were Jews to a man, that it was their own God, the God of Israel, who had now revealed himself in Jesus of Nazareth. The Epistle to the Hebrews expresses this feeling of continuity and culmination like this: 'God, who at sundry times and in divers manners spake in time past unto the fathers by the prophets, hath in these last days spoken unto us by his Son.'[1]

So the Old Testament is not just 'background' material for the earnest bible student, in the way that the Dead Sea Scrolls or the writings of the first century Jew Josephus are. It is not just a quarry for investigating the thought-forms of the New Testament. Nor is it just 'introduction': what the reader needs to know before he starts on Chapter One of the real story. No: the Old Testament is Volume I of a two-volume story, and each is indispensable for the proper understanding of the other. That is why the practice of printing and distributing New Testaments on their own is so dangerous. People read them, and think they know what they are about.

If then we desire to believe in the God of Jesus, we immediately find that what is asked of us is that we should believe in the God of Israel. For there is no God of Jesus except this God of Israel. The fact that we want to stand in the tradition of the apostles binds us to the tradition in which they stood: the tradition of the law and the prophets.

[1] Heb. 1.1f.

It is time now to ask more about this tradition. Who is—
or was—this God of Israel? Translate this question into
Hebrew, and it comes out in the form 'What is his *name*?'

Names play an important part in the Bible. In Hebrew
names have obvious meaning and associations, and people
were aware of them. They were more than the merely
distinguishing labels which our names usually are. Names
did not merely mark off A from B; they really said something about the nature of those who bore them. To take a
familiar New Testament example: Jesus renames Simon as
Cephas or Peter, 'Cephas' and 'Peter' being Aramaic and
Greek respectively for 'rock'. And, to take a recurrent Old
Testament example, the stories of the patriarchs are full of
incidents which turn on the meaning of their names.

This is first of all a cultural phenomenon. In many fairly
primitive societies a man's name is a kind of extension of
himself. To ask for someone's name is more than to ask for
his identifying label; it is to ask who he really is. Possession
of a man's name gives one, so to speak, internal and not
merely external knowledge about him. It therefore gives
one some kind of a hold over him. That is why in some
societies people have a real name which is kept secret, and
are known in ordinary conversation by periphrases or
substitute names. It is too dangerous to divulge one's real
name. Your enemies may make use of it, for instance by
writing it on bits of paper and setting fire to them.

The ancient Israelites did not have this practice of giving
themselves secret names. But they did regard the relationship
between a man and his name as being so close as almost to
be a relationship of identity. An example is God's promise
to Abraham: 'I will make of you a great nation, and I will

bless you, and make your name great.'[1] Here 'making Abraham's name great' clearly means little more than 'making Abraham great'.

But it was not only men who had names in the ancient Near East. So too did the gods. And it was equally, if not more, important to know their names. Knowing them, you knew something of the composition of the unseen world on which the life of men depended. Knowing the names of these powers, you could address them and hope for an answer; you could plead with them, and ask them to be kind. Magical texts are full of the names of the unseen powers, for it is the names that give one the power over them. A faint echo of this survives in the conjuror's 'Abracadabra' or in the 'Open Sesame!' of Ali Baba and the Forty Thieves. If you know the words, you can get the genie out of the bottle. But woe betide you if you don't know the words to get him back in again!

I said just now that in the world of old Israel the relationship between a man and his name was so close as almost to be one of identity. Strictly it is not a relationship of identity. Rather it is one of representation. The name represents its bearer—and in a stronger sense than that word usually suggests. It does more than represent; it re-presents. The name is a mediation of presence. This is of great importance when one comes to think about the gods. For if the name re-presents its bearer, then (in the biblical phrase) to 'call upon the name' of a god is in some sense to make him present. He is not identical with his name; but where his name is uttered, there there is a mediation of his presence.

Thus the name of a god has a very similar function to that

[1] Gen. 12.2.

of an image. The images of ancient gods, objects of wood or metal or stone, represented and re-presented the deities whose they were. Despite the polemic of the Israelite prophets, the nations were not so foolish as really to believe that the images were themselves gods. What they did believe was that in the images the deities made themselves present. And the holiest and most ancient images, like the famous image of Artemis at Ephesus, were not man made; they were given by heaven itself. The names and the images of the gods were thus points of communication with the beings they represented. The name functioned as a kind of audible image, the image proper as a visible or tangible one.

Both forms of image, the audible and the visible, played an important role in the religion of the peoples among whom ancient Israel lived. For that very reason, and in conscious reaction, the name and the image played an important even if largely negative role in the religion of Israel itself.

Israel was forbidden to make any image of its god. This imageless worship was one of the things about Judaism which caused astonishment in the ancient world. Both of Jerusalem's Roman conquerors, Pompey in 63 BC and Titus in AD 70, entered the Holy of Holies of the temple, presumably to see for themselves what the mystery was at the heart of the Jews' religion—and found nothing. For the God of Israel, alone among the gods of the ancient world, had no visible image in his temple.

He had no image; and while he certainly had a name, it was (as we shall see) a name of a peculiar kind. The utterance of the Name was the only form of representation of the deity that was allowed. No visible image; only the audible one which comes into being by being pronounced, and then dies away into silence. Furthermore, by the time of Jesus even the utterance of the Name was allowed only on a very few occasions, by the priests in the liturgy of the temple.

There is one part of the Old Testament in particular where there is reflection on this question of divine images and names. This is in the traditions connected with Moses and with the story of the self-revelation of Israel's God at Mount Sinai. Take for instance a passage in Deuteronomy in which Moses is recalling the events of Mount Sinai, and notice how it handles the motif of the audible in contrast to the visible self-manifestation of God. Moses is addressing Israel: 'And you came near and stood at the foot of the mountain, while the mountain burned with fire to the heart of heaven; and there was darkness, cloud, and thick darkness. And the LORD spoke to you out of the midst of the fire. You heard the sound of words, but saw no form; there was only a voice.'[1] All they heard was a voice—the voice of God's self-revelation. That (as we shall shortly see) is identical with his utterance of his own Name.

The close connection between the giving of this Name—the audible image—and the rejection of the visible or tangible image is clear from another passage, one which is at the very heart of the Sinai material. I refer to the opening sentences of the Ten Commandments. 'I am the LORD your God who brought you out of the land of Egypt, out of the house of bondage. You shall have no other gods before me. You shall not make for yourself a graven image, or any likeness of anything that is in heaven above, or that is in the earth beneath, or that is in the water under the earth; you

[1] Deut. 4.11f.

shall not bow down to them or serve them; for I the LORD your God am a jealous God.'[1]

To get to the point of this, you must remember one thing: that every time one sees the word LORD printed in capital letters in our English bibles, what in fact stands in the Hebrew is the divine name YHWH. This tradition of substituting LORD, or its Hebrew equivalent, for YHWH goes back to the custom of the synagogues. The Name was regarded as so sacred that wherever the reader came upon it in his reading of the Scriptures, he substituted for it the Hebrew word for 'Lord'.

Thus the Ten Commandments really begin: 'I am YHWH your God who brought you out of the land of Egypt.' The God of Israel is uttering his Name, revealing himself through that representation of himself which consists in his Name. The nature which the Name reveals in this way is such that the first two commandments necessarily follow from it. First, the Name makes an exclusive claim on the allegiance of those who invoke it: 'You shall have no other gods before me.' Secondly, since this Name is the all-sufficient image or representation of the God whose name it is, any other image one may try to make of him will only derogate from this. All other images are therefore excluded: 'You shall not make yourself a graven image, or any likeness of anything that is in heaven, or earth, or in the water under the earth; you shall not bow down to them or serve them.'

The force of all this will come out more clearly if we look at the passage where the Name is first revealed to Moses— the passage about the Burning Bush.

Moses is in the wilderness of Sinai looking after the flocks

[1] Exod. 20.2–5.

of his father-in-law Jethro. He comes to the mountain of God, that very same mountain where God later reveals himself to the whole people of Israel. He hears a voice calling him out of a bush which is strangely aflame and yet not burnt. 'I am the God of your father, the God of Abraham, the God of Isaac, the God of Jacob. . . . Come, I will send you to Pharoah that you may bring forth my people the children of Israel out of Egypt.'[1]

Then comes the crucial question. Moses asks, 'If I come to the children of Israel and say to them, "The God of your fathers has sent me to you", and they ask me, "What is his name?" What am I to say to them?'[2] The people will ask, 'What is his name?' By that they will mean: 'Who is he?'—and all that that implies. 'What is his character? What is he good for? How can we invoke him? Only if we know who he is will we be able to know when we can rely on him—and (for the same reason) when we can better call upon others. Tell us who he is, and we shall know whom we are dealing with. We shall know the words which bind even deity. We shall know how to summon the great genie. What is his name?'

The Name has been asked for, and it is given. Three times, each time put differently. First: 'God said to Moses, "I AM AS I AM".' Second: 'Say this to the children of Israel, "I AM has sent me to you".' And third: 'Say this to the children of Israel, "YHWH, the God of your fathers, the God of Abraham, the God of Isaac, and the God of Jacob, has sent me to you. This is my name for ever, and thus am I to be remembered throughout all generations".'[3] It is of course the third form of the answer which gives the Name

[1] Exod. 3.6, 10.   [2] Exod. 3.13.   [3] Exod. 3.14 f.

itself: YHWH. The other two forms, I AM and the more extended I AM AS I AM, are exegesis, explanation. They show what the faith of Israel understood to be the meaning of 'YHWH'.

How are we to understand it: this I AM, or I AM AS I AM? First let us briefly notice three points.

(1) The meaning of I AM AS I AM is not the banality 'I'm me' (as the usual translation 'I am who I am' may misleadingly suggest). Nor is it a petulant 'Shan't tell.' Yet again (and more important), neither does it strictly mean 'I am the existent one.' For the phrase is not so much concerned with God's mere existence as with his practical presence. Not so much 'Does he exist?' as 'Is he there?' So a useful alternative to the rendering 'I am' is 'I am there' or 'I am present.'

(2) The Hebrew tense system is such that these words can legitimately and properly be referred, as they were in later Jewish interpretation, to past, present, or future, or to all three at once: 'I was', 'I am', and 'I shall be.' The author of the Revelation of John in the New Testament tries to represent this in Greek when he has God declare, 'I am the Alpha and the Omega, says the Lord God, who is and who was and who is to come, the sovereign Lord of all.'[1]

(3) The shorter version of the Name (I AM) is qualified by the longer (I AM AS I AM); but this is not a qualification which limits its meaning. Rather it insists that it cannot be limited. And almost any English relative can legitimately be used to translate the connecting relative in Hebrew: 'I am as I am', 'I am who I am', 'I am where I am.' The qualifying

[1] Rev. 1.8.

phrase thus sets the bare I AM free from all limitation: I AM
AS I AM.

'What is his name?' the people will ask. Has their question
been answered? In one sense, yes. A name has been given.
But in another sense the answer is a refusal to give one—or
at any rate, it is a refusal to give an answer of the kind pre-
supposed by the question. The question asks for the name
because, having it, one will know whom one is dealing with;
one will have some hold over him whose name it is. But
this name is itself a refusal to give this kind of an answer. It
is a categorical refusal to be held down. It is an answer
which, in one sense, leaves the questioner in as great an
ignorance as he started in. No man knows who this God is.
For who is he? He who is as he is. There is the transcendence,
the freedom, the incomprehensibility of God.

But the No of the Name is nothing but the reverse side of
an astonishing Yes. God's refusal to be bound to guarantees
is the corollary of his freedom to bind himself to promises.
Guarantees have limits: in such and such circumstances I
undertake to do such and such. The promise given in the
Name is as boundless as the freedom which it also expresses:
I AM THERE and I WILL BE THERE, AS I WILL BE THERE.
How will he be known to be there? In the making and
keeping of this promise, as it clothes itself in particular
promises. We see this happening in this very passage.
Immediately after pronouncing the Name, the voice of God
continues: 'Go and gather the elders of Israel together, and
say to them, "YHWH, the God of your fathers, the God of
Abraham, of Isaac, and of Jacob, has appeared to me,
saying, I have surely observed you and what has been done

to you in Egypt; and I promise that I will bring you up out of the affliction of Egypt, to the land of the Canaanites, the Hittites, the Amorites, the Perizzites, the Hivites, and the Jebusites, to a land flowing with milk and honey!"'[1] Thus the promise is particularized, but in the freedom of the Name there is always room for more. Wherever his people are, there their God will be with them. That promise stands. *How* he will be with them, whether in terror or in mercy, that is for him to determine. No man has him in his power. But *that* he will be with them as their God, that he promises.

The promise of presence: that is the meaning of the Name. This understanding of the nature of Israel's God is expressed again and again in the Exodus stories. It is expressed by that symbol of the divine presence, the pillar of cloud by day and of fire by night, which accompanies the people on their way through the desert. It is expressed again when Moses says to God, 'How shall it be known that I have found favour in your sight, I and your people? Is it not in your going with us, so that we are distinct, I and your people, from all other people that are on the face of the earth?'[2] Finally there is the promise spelt out (and notice how the promise is grounded in the Name): 'If you walk in my statutes and observe my commandments and do them, then . . . I will set my abode among you, . . . and I will walk among you. And I will be your God, and you shall be my people. I am YHWH your God, who brought you forth out of the land of Egypt, that you should not be their slaves; and I have broken the bars of your yoke and made you walk upright.'[3]

[1] Exod. 3.16 f.   [2] Exod. 33.16.   [3] Lev. 26.3, 11 ff.

Once we have understood something of the meaning of the Name we can see still better why its announcement at the beginning of the Ten Commandments is immediately followed by the prohibition both of images and of the worship of any other gods.

First: images. If the Name is the all-sufficient representation of him whom it reveals precisely as the one who is present, then to ask for any other image or re-presentation is in fact to disbelieve in the Name. It is to doubt the promise of presence. That is why images are forbidden in Israel. That too is why, in contrast to other gods, this God has one name only. Not only are visible images excluded. So too are all audible images except this one. Marduk, the god of Babylon, for instance, had fifty names, each one to capture some aspect of his being which might not have been caught by the other forty-nine. The God of Israel has one name only, which declares itself to be all-sufficient. To ask for any others would be to disbelieve the one.

Secondly: 'You shall have no other gods before me.' This is not, strictly speaking, an enunciation of monotheism. In fact for the greater part of their history ancient Israel believed that other gods existed—for other nations. But for them there was to be one God only, and to him they must look for everything. For to look to others would be to suppose that there were limits to the limitless promise. It would be to disbelieve the Name.

The Name is the promise of presence. As we saw just now, this is a promise that utters itself in promises, that allows itself to be particularized. The Old Testament is filled with such particular promises: promises of freedom, of land, of children, promises of kings who will rule in justice, promises of peace, and of life from death. All are particularizations of 'I will be there as I will be there'; of 'I will be your God and you shall be my people.' It is only in the particular and the concrete that this general concept manifests itself, only in the particular that it can be experienced and known as true.

That is why, all the way through, there is such an emphasis on the particular. To take an example from the passage we were discussing (the Burning Bush), God does not only announce his Name, that he is YHWH, I AM. He clothes it in a promise of particular presence: 'I have seen the affliction of my people . . . and I have come down to deliver them.'[1] Furthermore this promised presence of the future is explicitly linked with the experienced presence of the past: 'I am the God of your father, the God of Abraham, the God of Isaac, and the God of Jacob.'[2] So again at the beginning of the Ten Commandments, a phrase which re-echoes throughout the Old Testament, 'I am YHWH your God, who brought you out of the land of Egypt, out of the house of bondage.'[3] It is still the same in the latest book of all, the book of Daniel. When Daniel has been saved from the den of lions, the great King Darius issues a decree that 'in all my royal dominion men tremble and fear before the God of Daniel . . . him who has saved Daniel from the power of the lions.'[4] All the way through he reveals his presence in particulars: the God of Abraham, of Isaac, and of Jacob, the God who delivered from Egypt, the God who saved Daniel from the lions.

Here then is belief in a god who commits himself to the revelation of his power and his presence in the concrete and the particular. It is precisely because of this that the agony

[1] Exod. 3.7 f.   [2] Exod. 3.6.   [3] Exod. 20.2.
[4] Dan. 6.26 f.

of his absence arises, when the evidence of the particular fails. We see this happening in the life of the individual— Job, for instance, the righteous man who keeps the commandments of God and yet from whose life all sign of the divine presence has failed. 'Behold, I go forward, but he is not there; and backward, but I cannot perceive him; on the left hand I seek him, but I cannot behold him; I turn to the right hand, but I cannot see him.'[1] The problem also arises in the life of the nation, most acutely in the sixth century BC when all the characteristic marks of God's presence and favour have been removed; king, temple and land have all been taken away.

This is the point where belief in the Name is put to its severest test. If you have a tolerant kind of a religion, it is not too difficult to cope with this kind of situation. The vicissitudes of human life are a mirror of the conflicts of heaven. If there's a drought, then the god of summer heat has got the upper hand over the god of rain and fertility; and when the rains return, then the roles have been reversed. So too if the King of Babylon or Assyria comes and reduces you to political subjection, making your king his vassal, this too is reflected on the heavenly plane. Your gods have been conquered by his and have become their vassals. Precisely this understanding of the state of affairs was expressed by the way in which the kings of Assyria used to set up the images and altars of their gods in the temples of the kings and cities they had conquered. One god's defeat was another one's victory.

But if you have one God only, who makes exclusive claims upon you, what are you to do when the signs of his

[1] Job 23.8 f.

power and presence are removed? This question arises especially when his Name declares him as him who is present. You don't have the option of fitting him into some larger pantheon, for that is to deny the all-sufficient Name, and so to deny him. You have only two alternatives: either to apostatize outright, and so to deny him explicitly; or else to hang on to him even in the dark, and to try to discover his presence in his absence. This is the work of the great prophets of Israel: that they took the Name of their God so seriously that they discerned his presence and his power in the very removal of the signs which he himself had given of his presence and his power. It was not the gods of Assyria and Babylon who were overwhelming him, taking away his gifts of king, temple and land. He was removing them himself, destroying the signs of his own grace. Through the prophets Israel came to discern the hand that once had led them in the hand which now struck them. 'He has bent his bow like an enemy, with his right hand set like a foe; and he has slain all the pride of our eyes in the tent of the daughter of Zion; he has poured out his fury like fire. . . . The Lord has scorned his altar, disowned his sanctuary; he has delivered into the hand of the enemy the walls of her palaces.'[1]

I should like to emphasize two things about this much-misunderstood notion of the wrath of God. First, it is a fundamentally hopeful doctrine. It declares that you can fall into the hands of no alien power. Even when you are carried into exile, out of the land of promise, the hands that carry you are still those which once brought you into the land—and which have power to bring you back, according to the nature disclosed in the Name. 'I am YHWH and there

[1] Lam. 2.4, 7.

is no other, I form light and create darkness, I make weal and create woe; I am YHWH who do all these things.'[1]

Secondly, this is the point at which Israel's faith becomes truly monotheistic. In early days, as we have seen, Israel was forbidden to worship other gods. But that said nothing about the gods themselves; in fact, each nation was believed to have its own god. But now that Israel had been overwhelmed by these nations, one could only do one of two things: either acknowledge that their gods had done the overwhelming, and thus deny YHWH; or assert that YHWH himself had overwhelmed his people, and thus deny the power of the gods of Babylon. And to deny their power was to deny their effective existence. It was, paradoxically, the experience of the absence of their God that drove Israel to the confession of his universal power and presence. The prophet who above all asserts this is the so-called second Isaiah, who worked in exile in Babylon. Significantly, it is among his words that one finds this striking saying: 'Truly, thou art a God that hidest thyself, O God of Israel, the Saviour.'[2]

Here then is something about the tradition of faith which lies behind Jesus. Jesus' God was this God of Israel, who had made himself known as the God of Abraham, Isaac, and Jacob, in promising them land and posterity, and in keeping his promises; who had revealed his power and his presence in delivering serfs from bondage and in giving them a good land to live in; whose presence was perceived by the prophets in the removal of the signs of his presence; and who had then restored his people to their land and to their city of Jerusalem, and thus shown that his promises still

[1] Isa. 45.7.   [2] Isa. 45.15.

B

stood—'O give thanks unto the LORD, for he is good: for his mercy endureth for ever.'[1]

But always there was a gap between promise and fulfilment, a gap of which men became increasingly aware. Quite apart from the unfulfilled overplus of the particular promises, there was the limitless promise of the Name itself. None of the particular promises, however marvellously fulfilled, could ever exhaust that ultimate promise which springs from the very nature of God himself: 'I will be your God and you shall be my people'; 'I AM AS I AM.'

The experience of this gap between promise and fulfilment was of course a form of the experience of God's absence. Out of it came a fierce longing for a fulfilment of the promises which would somehow be final, for a day when the gap between promise and fulfilment would be closed for good, and when their God would indeed and for ever make himself known as their God. This was a hope and a longing for an irremoveable fulfilment of the promise of presence, which is the promise of the Name. This looking for the 'hallowing of the Name'[2] is Israel's fundamental hope —a hope correlative to YHWH's fundamental promise—a hope which is classically expressed in the words of the Lord's Prayer: 'Thy Name be hallowed, Thy Kingdom come, Thy will be done, As in heaven so on earth.'

Just like the promise, this fundamental hope was articulated in particular hopes—hopes for a more or less cataclysmic interruption of history, when God would establish his kingdom of justice and of peace upon earth, when Israel would be saved from enemies without and sinners within, to serve their God with singleness of heart. One of these

[1] Ps. 136.1.   [2] Ezek. 36.23.

hopes was often the hope for a Messiah, an anointed king who would be God's agent in establishing this kingdom. But all these particular hopes—for a Messiah, for liberty, for peace and righteousness on earth—all are particularizations of this fundamental hope, that God will 'hallow his Name'.

If anything characterizes the spiritual climate of the Jews of Jesus' time, it is this hope and longing for the kingdom of God. God had made himself known to their fathers, and they longed the more for his kingdom in the future because he somehow seemed far distant in the present. The experience of God's present withdrawal expressed itself in many ways—for instance in the belief that prophecy was now silent, that there were no longer men who could say with an immediate authority, 'Thus says the LORD.' And the conviction arose that God in his immeasurable holiness and transcendence had no immediate dealings with the world, but that his action and presence were mediated by a host of angels and other beings. One spoke no longer of God directly, but of 'heaven', or 'the power', or 'the word', or 'the Name'. And the Name itself might no longer be pronounced, except by priests on specified occasions in the service of the temple —and then, according to one report, they were to mumble lest the people actually hear it.

What, when God thus appeared to have withdrawn himself, were the faithful to do? Keep the commandments, and hope and wait. One feels this atmosphere in the opening chapters of the Gospel according to Luke, with its picture of pious Israelites like Zechariah and Elizabeth, Simeon and Anna, keeping the commandments—and waiting.

This was the world in which Jesus was born. And what

does he have to say? 'The time is fulfilled. The Kingdom of God is upon you.'[1] God is no longer far away. His power and his presence are near. He is on the very point of making himself known in that final way which will transcend all that is past. His promises—all of them—are about to be fulfilled. There is no point at which Jesus makes his belief in the nearness of God clearer than in his teaching on prayer —and in his own practice of prayer. He addressed God simply as 'Abba' (Father), and instructed his disciples to do the same. No complicated or grand allocutions such as the heathen make, because they don't know who God is and have to try to catch him somehow. No, the disciples of Jesus are the true sons of Israel. They know who God is and are to address him simply as their Father who is present to hear them. Any more would be unbelief. In this teaching on prayer, Jesus is reiterating the ancient faith in the Name— God is present to hallow his Name: I AM THERE and I WILL BE THERE. Jesus staked his life on this belief—the belief that the God of Moses was still there to be *his* God, the God and Father of Jesus.

Now, in Jesus, this belief in God's presence and power was once more put to the test and tried in the fire of affliction. In what sense was God present at the crucifixion? What more God-forsaken scene than Golgotha: 'My God, my God, why hast thou forsaken me?'[2] What sign here of God's power to stand by his children? We hear the mockery of the priests: 'He trusted in God; let him deliver him now, if he will have him: for he said, I am the Son of God. The thieves also, which were crucified with him, cast the same in his teeth.'[3]

[1] Mark 1.15.   [2] Matt. 27.46.   [3] Matt. 27.43 f.

Once more, in this abandonment, a new dimension is revealed to the power and presence of God. It was, according to St Paul, precisely in the Cross that God's *power* was revealed. Jesus staked his life on his belief in God's power to fulfil the promise of his presence—and (according to the apostles) he won. What was the sign of his victory? Nothing less than resurrection from death. But this is a victory which can only be won through loss. Resurrection is something which can follow only on death. Here is power made known once again through weakness, presence revealed once more in absence. That, at least, is what the apostles believed and preached: that the faith of Jesus had been justified; that the God of Israel had indeed revealed himself once more—as the God of Jesus. 'God, who at sundry times and in diverse manners spake in time past unto the fathers by the prophets, hath in those last days spoken unto us by his Son.'[1] And so to the list of Old Testament characterizations they add another. Not only 'the God of Abraham, Isaac, and Jacob', 'the God who brought Israel out of Egypt', 'the God who saved Daniel from the lions', but also —characteristic and recurring phrase—'the God and Father of our Lord Jesus Christ'. In the life, death and resurrection of Jesus the God of Israel had again revealed his power and his presence. He was now the God 'who raised Jesus from the dead'.[2]

I should like to end with two New Testament texts, both of which refer to God's self-revelation through Jesus, and which, taken together, sum up that continuity I have been trying to point to. The first comes from the Song of Zechariah: 'Blessed be the Lord God of Israel, for he hath

[1] Heb. 1.1.   [2] Gal. 1. 1.1.

visited and redeemed his people.'[1] The second is from the First Letter of Peter: 'Blessed be the God and Father of our Lord Jesus Christ, which according to his abundant mercy hath begotten us again unto a lively hope by the resurrection of Jesus Christ from the dead.'[2] The God of Israel had made himself known as the God of Jesus Christ.

Christians believe in the God of Jesus, not only in the sense of belief in the God whom Jesus believed in, but also —and yet more important—they believe in the God who revealed his presence and power *as* the God of Jesus—as 'the God and Father of our Lord Jesus Christ'.

[1] Luke 1.68.   [2] 1 Pet. 1.3.

3

THE GOD OF THE CHRISTIANS

BY

G. W. H. LAMPE

'FATHER, hallowed be thy name. Thy kingdom come. Give us day by day our daily bread; and forgive us our sins, for we ourselves forgive every one who is indebted to us; and lead us not into temptation.' Like the Hebrew prophets and wise men whose belief he inherited, Jesus, so far as we know, never addressed himself to the kind of question that asks who, or what, God is, or what we mean when we use the word 'God'. The Gospels contain no attempt to explain that word. They do not seem to be interested in what is now our major theological problem. Instead, they speak about what God does and what we may hope and trust that he will do, God's existence being taken for granted. The words I have quoted, St Luke's version of the 'Lord's Prayer', are an example of the way in which very early tradition reported Jesus to have spoken about God.

Later Christian thought has been less reticent about the being, as opposed to the activity, of God. The first of the Thirty-Nine Articles is a comparatively simple assertion: 'There is but one living and true God, everlasting, without body, parts or passions; of infinite power, wisdom and goodness; the Maker and Preserver of all things both visible and invisible. And in unity of this Godhead there be three Persons, of one substance, power, and eternity; the Father, the Son and the Holy Ghost.' The so-called Creed of St Athanasius (not properly a creed, having no direct

61

connection with St Athanasius; otherwise well-named) offers a much more elaborate definition. 'The Catholic Faith is this: that we worship one God in Trinity, and Trinity in Unity; neither confounding the persons, nor dividing the substance. For there is one person of the Father, another of the Son, and another of the Holy Ghost. But the Godhead of the Father, of the Son, and of the Holy Ghost, is all one, the glory equal, the majesty co-eternal. Such as the Father is, such is the Son, and such is the Holy Ghost. . . . For like as we are compelled by the Christian verity to acknowledge every Person by himself to be God and Lord; so are we forbidden by the Catholic Religion to say, There be three Gods or three Lords. The Father is made of none: neither created, nor begotten. The Son is of the Father alone: not made, nor created, but begotten. The Holy Ghost is of the Father and the Son: neither made, nor created, nor begotten, but proceeding. . . . And in this Trinity none is afore, or after other: none is greater, or less than another: but the whole three Persons are co-eternal together, and co-equal. So that in all things, as is aforesaid, the Unity in Trinity and the Trinity in Unity is to be worshipped. He therefore that will be saved must thus think of the Trinity.' Clearly, the thinking which produced this kind of theological statement is very different indeed from that which finds expression in the Lord's Prayer (though it is worth noticing that the context of both is, up to a point, similar: 'When you *pray*, say "Father . . ."'; 'the Catholic Faith is that we *worship* one God . . .').

Now, in making this contrast between two quite different kinds of language about God I am not suggesting that the elaborate dogmatic formulation is worthless: still less that it is ridiculous. On the contrary, the meaning of doctrinal statements such as the creeds and other historical professions of belief, the circumstances which evoked them, and the philosophical presuppositions which helped to determine the character of their assertions are all matters of the greatest interest and importance. It would be altogether superficial (it would, in fact, be anachronistic) to say 'Jesus never asked anyone to believe a creed' (that, as a matter of fact, although often said, is scarcely true—see Mark 12.28). 'The Church got to work on the simple faith of Jesus in the God of Israel, and built it up into a crazy structure of unverifiable metaphysical assertions. Let us ignore all these artificial constructions and get back to the simplicity of the "Our Father".' Of course, no one could deny that in the process of theological elaboration something has certainly happened to the God of Jesus. The God of Christian theology is by no means the same. But this does not necessarily mean that the process of reflection upon the God of Jesus, in the light of different philosophies and within the framework of different cultures, through which the Christian God, or rather the varying Christian ideas of God, have taken shape, has been a mere waste of time or that we can afford to ignore it. I want to say something about the way in which reflection upon Jesus' own faith in God led to the historic formulations of orthodox Christianity, and why these doctrinal constructions are important, both because of what they positively affirm and because we cannot revise or replace them unless we understand what they were intended to do.

In trying to do this I must put in one or two preliminary warnings. The whole process of the development of Christian thought has been hampered by the simultaneous growth of certain major errors. One of these is the tendency to think that truths about God have been revealed to men 'neat', as it were. I mean, communicated from a divine source by Jesus Christ as God, through inspired prophets and wise men, apostles, teachers, the writers of the books of the Bible, councils of church leaders, popes, and so on, in such a way that the message has been transmitted in human language, clothed in the external forms of human thought, given, indeed, in the characteristic language and thought-forms of particular nations and cultures, but at the same time in such a way that its essential content has been unaffected by the human mind's fallibility, ignorance and feebleness of apprehension. It is not just, as it is often said to be, that revelation is given in things that happen and does not consist of propositions. I think that this is a true statement about revelation; and it is also partly true that when Christians speak of 'faith' they mean primarily 'faith in' or 'trust in' someone: in God, who is personal, in Jesus Christ. There *is* a very important difference between personal faith or trust, and 'the Faith' as a body of propositions. So it is worth noticing that the Apostles' Creed begins, 'I believe *in* God' and continues, 'And *in* Jesus Christ'. There is a very significant difference between this affirmation of personal trust and the statement of the Athanasian Creed that 'the right faith is that we believe and confess *that* our Lord Jesus Christ, the Son of God, is God and Man'. Yet too much can be made of this distinction. To believe or trust *in* someone necessarily involves having certain beliefs *about* him, beliefs which can be expressed in propositions. So, too, events, in which we may find revealed to us something or someone in whom we are impelled to put our trust, are revelatory only in so far as we react to them in certain special ways. My point is simply that there is no form of revelation which is not given and received in and through the human reason, imagination and emotions. You can never isolate an activity of God in such a way as to be able to demonstrate that it is God's activity and nothing else: so as to point to it and say 'Here, plainly and unmistakably, God is at work. Here is something which is explicable only by reference to God.' The mistaken hope that something like this can, after all, be done has caused much confusion and misunderstanding in respect of miracles. The fact that it cannot be done creates some of those difficulties for Christian belief which were discussed in Mr Baelz's lecture. But the divine cannot be isolated for identification and examination.

A most central affirmation of Christian belief is the divinity of Jesus. This does not mean that Jesus is not a man; Christians are generally glad to say, 'Jesus is God'; they are not willing to speak of 'the God Jesus'. Nor does it mean that in some respects he is divine and in other respects he is human, though theologians have sometimes talked as if that were the case: as though Jesus played a double role, appearing on the stage now as God, now as man, switching over from the one to the other. Divinity, whatever precisely we may mean by it, is mediated in and through this man's humanity. One may express it as a further dimension in which his human character is set, or as a peculiar perspective in which that human character is seen. It has to do with a quality, discernible in that human character, which confronts us with a claim to our worship: in response to which it is not absurd, as it would be in the case of other men, to exclaim 'My Lord and my God'. It is like this with revelation. It cannot be isolated and examined apart from the human reasoning and imagination through which it is mediated. It is very easy, and quite false, to interpret the person of Jesus docetically: that is, to suppose that he is God walking about this earth got up to look like a man but not in fact truly human at all. It is equally easy and false to take a docetic view of revelation: to suppose that the content of the scriptures, for example, is, just simply, the thoughts of God, the human writers contributing no more than a pen for God to write them down with; or to imagine that a person or a group of people or an institution can, as it were, throw a switch from time to time and become a transmitter of revelation from an external divine source: a group of bishops, for instance, when assembled in council, or a pope when defining a dogma *ex cathedra*. It is not that revelation is a meaningless concept, nor that in fact no revelation is ever given; but rather that however we may experience it, in the 'givenness' of truth, of the insights of great art, of poetry and of worship, it can never be authenticated as revelation by any criteria external to itself. It cannot be demonstrated to be revelation to those to whom it has not already authenticated itself: those to whom it *is* not already revelation. Nor is it exempt from misunderstanding and distortion through the fallibility and inadequacy of human understanding. There can, therefore, be no infallible under-standing of the truth, nor any presentation of it which is guaranteed inerrant. No doctrinal statement or moral judg-ment of any kind is privileged in this respect. Scripture, tradition, creeds, councils, fathers, magisterium of the Church: none of them possesses guaranteed infallibility. Nor, I think, would the sayings of Jesus, even if they were recorded by the evangelists verbatim, exactly as spoken. We have to live in all respects by faith and not by certainty. And I interpret the New Testament as showing that this was also true of Jesus himself. That wonderful, deep, unbroken fellowship with God which stands out in the Gospels as the root-principle of his life is the perfect expression of faith, which trusts absolutely, but which does not know what all the answers will be.

The mistaken belief that we can have access to divinely guaranteed revelation, communicated to us by some infallible authority, is the root cause of another major error which accompanied the process of Christian theological reflection. This is the tendency for orthodoxy to replace faith, and consequently for the conviction to arise that it is by professing 'the faith' as a system of beliefs, rather than by trusting in God, that men come to be acceptable to him. So the Athanasian Creed begins: 'Whosoever will be saved, before all things it is necessary that he hold the Catholic Faith.' It then sets out the Catholic Faith in a series of theological affirmations, and it ends: 'This is the Catholic Faith, which except a man believe faithfully, he cannot be saved.' There is a very important contrast between this statement and the answer which Paul and Silas gave when they were asked the question, 'What must I do to be saved?' Their answer was, 'Believe in the Lord Jesus and you will be saved.' There is a great difference, too, between Thomas's cry of adoration, 'My Lord and my God', and the Christological definition in the Thirty-Nine Articles: 'The Son which is the Word of the Father, begotten from everlasting of the Father, the very and eternal God, and of one substance with the Father, took man's nature in the womb of the Blessed Virgin, of her substance, so that two whole and perfect natures, that is to say, the Godhead and the Manhood, were joined together in one Person, never to be divided, whereof is one Christ, very God and very man.' But this difference, I repeat, does not imply that it was a mistake to formulate an elaborate doctrinal definition such as the one I have just quoted. The mistake consists in supposing that formulations of this kind are either directly revealed by God or composed out of divinely guaranteed statements in creeds or scripture, and that they are therefore perfect, inerrant and unchangeable: and therefore that man's salvation turns on whether or not he assents to them. Assent to theological systems is not the faith by which we are justified. The history of the Church shows us all too plainly the dreadful consequences of this identification of a static orthodoxy with faith in God through Jesus Christ. Yet it tells us equally clearly that even supposedly infallible definitions have never been able permanently to act like a sort of straitjacket on the living and developing faith of Christian people. *Ecclesia semper reformanda* (The Church is always to be reformed): and the need for the Church to be continually reformed and renewed extends to the nature of its actual belief in God. For genuine belief cannot be static. It has to live and grow and change, both in content and in expression.

The traditional formulations of doctrine, then, are not irreformable. Nor, on the other hand, should we be wise if we were simply to tear them up: not even if our object were to try to go back, anachronistically, to the God of Jesus. Christian theology is an attempt to follow up, as it were, the ongoing process of development of the faith by which, as a matter of ascertainable fact, Christian people do actually live. Their outlook, way of life, special concerns, worship and prayer constitute the raw material for the Christian theologian. He tries to analyse all this and to give a rational account of it. At no time can he expect his account to be complete and exhaustive. At best it will always be inadequate, since it is an attempt to speak about an experience of the transcendent, and to offer a rational interpretation of what is necessarily mysterious, elusive, and in the last resort scarcely expressible. All that the theologian says is therefore highly tentative and provisional. St Augustine recognised that in discoursing at length about the ineffability of the Trinity he was trying only to make people understand that nothing can be said about it at all. He also explained that the Trinitarian formula, 'three Persons', had been arrived at, not because of its value as a positive assertion but simply in order to avoid having nothing to say at all. The same sort of attitude has to be taken towards most theological affirmations. They resemble to some extent the models used in other fields of enquiry. They are valuable so long as they help to interpret our experience as Christian people and to indicate the direction in which we ought to look if we want to understand something of the nature of our belief.

They must, on the other hand, be subject to modification; and circumstances may arise in which models which were once of the greatest value may cease to be helpful and have to be discarded altogether. In principle, I think, this applies to all doctrinal formulations, including such basic articles as that of the Trinity (that the one God is in three Persons), or the Incarnation (that the eternal Son of God was made man).

F

It is worth bearing in mind that the most orthodox Christian theology has always recognised, in one sense, that its assertions have this provisional and partial character. For it has maintained that God is indefinable and incomprehensible, beyond all the categories of thought. God can be spoken of only in negative terms; we can say only what God is not, using predicates which begin in Greek with the prefix α, and in English with 'in-' and 'un-'. We cannot even venture to say that God is: for God transcends being itself. Anything positive that we may say about God is not to be understood univocally; we can use only the language of analogy, and it is within a bracket, as it were, which is governed by a negative sign that all theology is enclosed.

Of course, it is not at all easy to determine who should pronounce on whether a theological model has outlived its usefulness or is showing signs of obsolescence, or by what criteria the matter should be decided. There have been times when such decisions have been made by large sections of the Christian community—whole churches—collectively, under the influence of leading thinkers. One such occasion was when the sixteenth-century reformers replaced unsatisfactory definitions of divine grace: models and analogies which seemed misleading because they offered an inadequate or untrue expression and interpretation of the Christian experience of God's gracious approach to man; they did not clearly indicate that by 'grace' is meant 'God being gracious'. More often the process of revision and renewal seems to be more gradual. Some individuals find it necessary to modify or discard the ancient confessions of belief, while the Church as a whole continues to be able to assert them in their original form and in the sense in which they were first drawn up; or, the majority may gradually abandon them while certain individuals continue to find them useful and to cherish them. Situations of this sort are very often to be met with at the present time. They create an appearance of confusion and uncertainty, and many people, especially those who observe the situation of the churches from the outside, find this uncertainty and confusion shocking or ridiculous. As for Christians, it certainly puts a strain on their tolerance and charity; for the scrapping and replacing of models may be a painless affair in other fields of enquiry, where no ultimate commitment is engaged and no personal security is involved: where, in fact, no one specially *minds*. But formulations of belief do matter profoundly. People really care about what these statements are trying to say; and it is very hard for someone who finds a traditional pattern meaningful and satisfying to recognise that fellow-Christians who may have ceased to find it helpful are not being perverse and have not lost their faith. Especially is this so, as long as there remains a certain hangover from the not so distant past when orthodoxy was virtuous, doubt was appalling, and heresy was morally wicked. If, then, without being repelled by the wide range of disagreement and uncertainty among Christian people, we ask questions about their idea of God, we shall expect to receive diverse answers. We shall also discover that both consciously and unconsciously they have been continually modifying, developing and revising their idea of God all down the centuries, and are still doing so now.

I have spent a lot of time labouring this very obvious point, because although it is obvious it is important. Now we can look at what Christians were doing when they modified and developed Israel's idea of God and the way in which, according to their own tradition, Jesus himself had spoken about God. Of course, to do this properly would be to produce a detailed history of Christian thought during the nineteen centuries in which theology has been grappling with the problem of relating the God *of* Jesus to the God *in* Jesus. All I can try to do now is to remind you that the process of reflection upon the God of Jesus, by which I mean upon the good news announced by Jesus, that the kingdom of God is at hand, was begun and carried on by people whose thinking was determined by the fact that they belonged to a particular community. This society existed, among other things, in order to 'follow' or 'imitate' Jesus. And its members believed that they were called to do this because, as a group and as individuals, they were potentially capable of sharing in that special and central characteristic of the life of Jesus: his free, confident and intimate relationship with God—sonship. They spoke of, and to, God as 'our Father', believing that their confidence to approach God as sons and not as slaves was derived from, and made possible through, the peculiar intimacy with which they believed Jesus to have spoken of God as 'my Father', and addressed him by the familiar and homely children's word, 'Abba'. They believed that they, as a group, could 'have the mind of Christ', that is, an attitude of trust, dependence and obedience towards God, prompted by an inspiration which they called the Holy Spirit or the Spirit of Christ: an attitude which expressed itself towards other people in selfless, disinterested, Christ-like love. They knew themselves to be called to live in the Spirit of Christ. They believed this to be possible for them because, through their conviction that he had been raised from death, they did not simply look back in memory to Jesus, a dead preacher. They looked to him as the Lord, the present Lord, the saviour who had reconciled them to God, and the present, living, sovereign source of the inspiration and power which was transforming their outlook and reproducing his character in themselves. St Paul's startling way of describing this Christian experience was to speak of being 'in Christ'. It involved emancipation from self-centred preoccupation of all kinds, freedom from the tyranny of legalistic and pharisaical religion and morality, forgiveness, a new relation of sonship towards God, consecration to membership of a people called to serve his purposes for the world.

The good news preached by Jesus therefore became necessarily, good news about Jesus himself. For the faith of the community arose from, and was centred upon, the conviction that in the life of Jesus, and especially in the death and resurrection of Jesus, God was at work, decisively and uniquely. This is the basic conviction which determined the lines on which Christians developed their idea of God. The divinity of Jesus Christ—this is still the central affirmation of Christian faith. But this can be expressed in many different ways, using a variety of images and analogies. For myself, I understand the affirmation of Christ's divinity to mean that Jesus lived in a unique closeness to God, in an unbroken assurance of sonship, and with a total response of trust in God's Fatherhood; that this fact requires us to believe that he reflects God to us—God who is love—as fully and completely as God can be mirrored in human terms; that in his words and deeds God addresses us and encounters us; that the New Testament's picture of Jesus is the primary reference point for our attempts to say what we mean by the word 'God'; and that in our experience of meeting Christian people that picture is confirmed, in so far as we recognise in them the character, or Spirit, of Jesus: the distinctive notes of sonship and brotherhood.

But, as I said, this sort of belief can be expressed and understood in various ways; and this was already being done in the period of the New Testament itself. Jesus is called 'Son of God', sometimes in the sense of a man chosen and called to be a servant or agent of God and a special recipient of God's love and favour. So, in the Old Testament, the people of Israel is called 'son of God', and so is the king who represents and personifies the nation. Sometimes, to lay more emphasis on the uniqueness of this 'sonship' of Jesus, his birth and infancy, which would seem in fact to have been ordinary and obscure (his home and family were so ordinary that his fellow-townsmen would not accept him as a preacher in their synagogue), were pictured as having been miraculous and attended by wonders and glory. They were imagined as having literally fulfilled certain Old Testament texts in a way which showed that the scriptures, rightly understood, pointed to Jesus. Another way of speaking of his unique sonship was to say that Jesus had been predestined in the eternal purposes of God; in God's mysterious counsels Jesus had been designated from the beginning to do God's saving work. And, by a significant transference of the idea of predestination to another category of explanation, Jesus was sometimes thought of as actually pre-existent: not merely as having existed, as it were, in the foreknowledge and intention of God, but as a divine or heavenly being who had existed in another dimension before his human birth.

According to this interpretation he is the Son of God in another, very different, and as we should say more mythological sense: a Son who was with God and who was sent into the world, who, as the Nicene Creed says, 'came down from heaven and was incarnate . . . and was made man'. Along this line of interpretation we are approaching the great change in thought from 'Son of God' to 'God the Son', which was to come later. It is a form of explanation which made use of the ancient concept of God's Wisdom, pictured almost as a distinct personal entity, God's agent in the creation of the world and his intermediary towards his rational creatures, who enters into the souls of men and makes them the friends of God. As St Paul said, 'Christ the wisdom of God and the power of God'. In another closely related picture, Christ is the Word of God, God's address to man, the communication of God's thought, the mode of God's approach to his world, and, in accordance with the language of contemporary philosophy, the embodiment of that divine reason which permeates the cosmos, or the intermediary divine link between God and his creatures, the mode in which the transcendent God becomes immanent in the rational creation.

These are only some among the many pictures which Christians were already using in the first century to express their belief that God encountered men through the acts and words of Jesus; that in the end it was not merely possible but necessary to say that Jesus is God, not only that he is the image or mirror of God; and that Christians may and should pray to God through him (which means, to pray to God as made known in Jesus) and even pray to Jesus as God. They believed that the God of Israel had fulfilled his promises at this point in time; that his presence had drawn near to men; that through the man Jesus the love of God had reached out to men, accepting them as sons (through no merit of their own), transforming them into new people; that therefore it was right and proper to ascribe the work of Jesus to God, to see in his person 'God with us'. Indeed, it was *only* at this point in history, so the early Christians believed, that it had become possible to discern the true significance of the purposes and promises of the God of Israel. In the light of this disclosure the hopes and aspirations of the ancient prophets took on a new significance. Men saw in the work of Jesus a realisation of the prophets' vision of God's judgment and mercy; and in the light of this the thought of the prophets was seen to have pointed beyond the events of their own day and to have been fulfilled in Jesus: so that without Jesus it would have remained incomplete and been, as it were, left hanging in the air. So the Old Testament was read as a book about Jesus, though written before the event.

The Christians went further than this. They believed that it was only in and through Jesus that any true understanding and experience could be gained of God's attitude towards man and of the relationship into which God wished to bring men towards himself. Through his works in nature, as St Paul said, it is possible to apprehend God's 'eternal power and deity'. He meant that it is possible to read off from the world around us the truth that nature is not the ultimate reality. To worship nature is idolatry; and idolatry means that in the last resort man is at best worshipping himself, or some ideal projection of himself, for this is the highest object of worship that the natural order affords. So idolatry debases man and degrades him. But although nature itself should encourage man to discern power and deity which transcend it, it is only through Jesus' life, death and resurrection that man can be reconciled to God and become a son of God. All that Christians wanted to say about God thus had its central point of reference in Jesus. It was focused on him for he is the image, or reflection, of the invisible God. He discloses the nature of God. He is like God; God is like him; he is God for us; he is God.

It was along a line of thought such as this (though I realise that I am grossly over-simplifying a complex and subtle process of reflection on the part of the Christian community) that the dominant problem for theology in the early centuries came to be how to assert that Jesus is our Lord, and hence, since Lordship implies worship and it is idolatry to worship man, how to assert his deity. It was an exceedingly difficult problem because it had to be solved without denying the Hebrew monotheism which had been the faith of Jesus himself, without denying the historical truth of his life and death, and so without turning him into a divine being who was not really man at all, but God, or a god, dressed up in a human body. And it could not be solved, once Christianity had spread into the main stream of Greco-Roman thought, without taking full account of, and, to a considerable extent, coming to terms with, the basic presuppositions of Hellenistic theology. This last aspect of the problem was important. Christian faith believed in 'God with us': God not merely reflected through, but mediated in, a human life with all the limitations of genuine manhood; God incarnate and entering into the human condition, even to the point of suffering and death. In the main stream of Christian thought this descent, as it were, of the divine to share in our human existence was conceived in substantial rather than dynamic terms. To say that Jesus is a man so totally possessed by the Spirit of God that all his activity bears the stamp of divinity seemed inadequate. It suggested that God's Word had come to Jesus, and God's Spirit had moved him, in the same kind of way, though to an almost incomparably higher degree, in which the word of God came to the prophets and God's Spirit inspired them. Orthodox Christians did not want to say that Jesus was like an inspired prophet or saint, even a saint always and in all respects led and motivated by the grace of God. This would seem to detract from the uniqueness which they felt bound to ascribe to him. It would also make it difficult to say what they wanted to say about the salvation of man. If man needed to be set free from his self-centredness, liberated from demonic forces that held him prisoner, brought into a right relationship to God as a son to a Father, and, which is the same thing, saved from sin, then only God could meet his need. It was difficult to believe that a man, even if he were in the fullest possible sense a man of God, could save man. I am inclined to think that Christians tended to be misled by the anthropomorphic ideas of God with which, quite rightly up to a point, they often operated; and that they found it unnecessarily difficult to think of salvation being effected by the personal Spirit of God reaching out to men in judgment, mercy, forgiveness and love through the medium of a human personality. In the fifth century Christian orthodoxy formally rejected something rather like this interpretation of the divinity of Jesus, labelling it the Nestorian heresy; but I think it has much to teach us. How-

ever, the main stream of theology preferred to think of
Jesus Christ as a divine person, one who was not the bearer
of God's Word but was, ontologically, the Word or Son,
one who was God concretely manifested.

But the essence of the Hellenistic idea of God is that deity
is by nature all that men by nature cannot be: God is un-
compounded, absolutely simple, hence static (a state identified with perfection), unchanging, subject to no variation,
eternal, impassible, unmoved. How, then, could entry into
the human condition, and, more especially, suffering, be
predicated of one who is God? Besides this paramount
philosophical difficulty there was also to some extent a
further source of perplexity. Christians have always found
it hard, especially, perhaps, in popular devotion, to believe
that Jesus really reflects and mediates the reality of God at
the point where St John made the paradox so plain that
Jesus was 'glorified': in the humility of his self-giving love;
in the nakedness and helplessness of the Cross. It has always
seemed much easier to think of that sordidness and humilia-
tion not as a revelation of the true and actual glory of God,
but as a disguise in which the glory of God was temporarily
concealed. For Christians have been very ready to assume
that the best way to picture God is as an infinitely magnified
Caesar. You may remember that the words of the first of
the Anglican Articles, which I quoted at the beginning of
this lecture, list three attributes of God: power, wisdom,
goodness. Love is not among them; and it is significant that
power comes first. If one starts with this imperial image of
God it is hard to identify the man of Nazareth, who had
nowhere to lay his head, with God.

So the early Church was torn between its conviction that

Jesus was God and its reluctance to say that God could be Jesus. It sought a solution of the problem by way of personifying the concepts of God's Word and God's Wisdom, identifying, as I said just now, Word and Wisdom with a pre-existent Son of God, and asserting that it was this divine being, this personal projection or offspring of the mind and purpose of God who took human nature and lived and died and rose from death. It was not until nearly four centuries had passed that Christians as a whole were prepared to believe, and to express their belief in the Nicene Creed, that the Son or Word of God is none other than absolute and ultimate God: not an intermediary divine being; not God at one remove; not God at a lower level of divine being. But when this belief had been formulated it was no longer possible to fend off the scandal of the incarnation and the crucifixion by saying, in effect, that these things had happened to the Son of God, and that that is a different matter from happening to God. Of course, once the fender had been removed by the Nicene declaration that the Son of God is of the same substance or essence as the Father, the same problem was transferred to the question of the person of Christ. If in Jesus Christ we encounter one who is divine in the fullest sense—if he is the Son or Word of God who is of one and the same essence as God the Father—if he is 'God the Son'—then can we also see in him one who is truly human, of one and the same essence as ourselves in respect of his manhood, as the council of Chalcedon expressed it? That council tried to answer the problem in the terms in which fifth-century Christians asked it. It spoke of two complete and perfect natures, divine and human, concurring in the one Person of God the Son. Today the question would not be asked in the same terms, and the ancient answer, framed in the concepts of contemporary philosophy, is of little direct help to us. But Christians still want to say what the old creeds, definitions and articles of religion were striving in their own way to assert. They, I think it must be admitted, tended in some respects to produce confusion. They started from the conviction that God's creative love, his gracious dealing with his creatures, his purpose to bring men into true sonship towards himself whatever it might cost to win them over from complacent, hard-hearted, self-love, and his willingness to pay, himself, whatever it might cost—that all this was focused in the real, historical and human Jesus. They believed that in this person and at this point in history the God who is never far from each one of us is disclosed in such a way as to evoke our response of trust and faith. And in order to give an intelligible account of that conviction Christians were led by their inheritance of Hebraic and Hellenistic theology to speak of Jesus as the Second Person, incarnate, of the triune God—triune, because they also wished to affirm that the new quality of life within the Christian brotherhood, life in which the character of Jesus was in a measure reproduced, was itself an operation of God with them and possessing them: the Holy Spirit. But, having constructed this theology in order to interpret the data of Christian history and experience, they tended to let the metaphysic take charge: to develop, as it were, a momentum of its own. And so, instead of the metaphysic fitting and interpreting the facts (by which I mean what was known of the historical Jesus), the facts were sometimes distorted in order to fit the metaphysic. Thus, when Jesus had been identified with God the Son, of one substance with the Father, it became hard to take seriously those parts of the Gospels which recorded that he had experienced temptation, ignorance, conflict of desire with duty, and so on. Also, the process of abstract theological construction tended to be carried forward, again by its own momentum, to a point where abstraction led to meaninglessness. Having set out to assert distinctions within the unity of God in order to account for their beliefs about Jesus and the Holy Spirit, theologians then found it necessary to emphasise that they were still thinking in strictly monotheistic terms, not in the tritheistic fashion which has often characterised popular devotion with its half-concealed idea of what the late Bishop Pike used to call a 'committee God'. So they asserted that in the operation of each Person there is an act of the whole Trinity; that the Persons are distinguishable only in respect of their individual modes of subsistence: that the Son is God *qua* begotten, or God in the mode of filiation; that the Holy Spirit is God *qua* proceeding, or God in the mode of procession. I gave you some examples of this type of abstract theologising earlier on from the Athanasian Creed. I do not want to suggest that these concepts are ridiculous, but I do not myself find them meaningful and I do not think they throw any real light on what Christians believe, as a matter of conviction, about God.

But behind all these tendencies towards theological confusion there remains the fact that Christians continue to want to affirm what it was that the sometimes arid and abstract formulations were basically trying to say. And in the complex and sometimes tedious process of controversy, and attempts to pin down the incomprehensible and define the indefinable, we can discern a vigorous and constantly renewed effort to interpret the meaning of an overwhelm-ingly strong and transforming faith. To make that faith one's own has always been a very different matter from assenting to the ill-grounded abstractions of some Christian theologies. What it means can be best conveyed in those ancient images of turning from darkness to light, of death and resurrection, of new birth and re-creation. It is sym-bolically dramatised in sacraments: in self-abandonment to nothingness and to a figurative extinction, and then a rising to new life in the Spirit of Jesus, in baptism; in communion in the life of Jesus which was surrendered to destruction and dereliction in obedience to the will of God, and raised from death to be the life of his people, in the Lord's Supper. This faith learns of the love of God from Jesus and discovers from him that it evokes self-sacrifice for the sake of God's world and for one's individual neighbour. It discovers also in Jesus a call to a life of daily dying in order to receive life: the way of the Cross. The Christians' God is encountered in the active business of caring and concern, in the practical working out of obedience to God's kingdom, with its immense social and individual implications, and in the wor-ship and prayer which is at once a focal point in the life of sonship to God and also an aid to the realisation of sonship and brotherhood in daily living.

4

PRAYING

BY
JOHN DRURY

A WORD of preamble and warning: most, if not all, of the material in this lecture comes from the realms of the personal and the aesthetic. I don't think one need apologise for drawing on the personal, but the aesthetic does not seem to have achieved such a respectable place in theological discourse. I will be using a good deal of poetry, referring to a musical work from the literary point of view, and the way an artist works will come into consideration. So let me try to say a word about this.

First, these things are meant only as signposts or pointers suggesting, as Balthasar says, the direction in which to look for what is specifically Christian.

Secondly, still following Balthasar, they are nevertheless valid pointers. He says 'Just as in love I encounter the other *as* the other in all his freedom, and am confronted by something which I cannot dominate in any sense, so in the aesthetic sphere, it is impossible to attribute the form which presents itself to a fiction of my imagination. In both cases the "understanding" of that which reveals itself cannot be subsumed under categories of knowledge which imply control.'[1] In other words there is a simple and basic 'being there' about these things which makes them particularly appropriate in talk about the mysterious business of prayer.

It may well seem to you that it takes me rather a long time

[1] H. U. von Bathasar, *Love Alone*, Burns & Oates.

to get going, if I get going at all. So I will ask you to be patient and to bear in mind the words of Quince the weaver in his role of prologue in *A Midsummer Night's Dream*:

> Gentles, perchance you wonder at this show
> But wonder on till truth make all things plain.

Indeed, I hope you'll wonder on long after I have done.

'Theological work', said Karl Barth, 'does not merely begin with prayer and is not merely accompanied by it, in its totality it is peculiar and characteristic of theology that it can be done only in the act of prayer.'[1] It has been the declared policy of these lectures to be personal. We have tried to set before you the Jewish–Christian tradition as it is for us today. In doing that we have considered how it was for other people in other times. In all this the category of the personal, the fact of the individual set in his particular time and his particular community, has been our first concern. For this tradition has been constantly renewed, taking on new energies and new insights as it passes through the living experience of people. It has not gone through history like an express train, leaving the country on either side indifferent after the slight momentary disturbance. It has taken on the forms and styles of the people who have become engaged with it, and not just the forms and styles but the deepest convictions and perplexities too. Again and again it has been found that when men deal with this tradition faithfully and honestly, being the men they are and caught in the time which is theirs, then it comes alive; and the tradition itself is like the grain of wheat which falls into the ground, losing itself so as to spring up and bear fruit. It is only by

[1] *Evangelical Theology*, Fontana.

taking ourselves and our place and time seriously that the God of the Exodus, the God of Jesus, the God of the Fathers, can be our God too, and that we can recognise him. That is how it was for Augustine in a conversion which was a re-discovery of a 'beauty at once so ancient and so new'. 'How was it', he wondered, 'that I recognised them [the Christian facts] when they were mentioned and agreed that they were true? It must have been that they were already in my mem-ory, hidden away in its deepest recesses, in so remote a part of it that I might not have been able to think of them at all, if some other person [Monica, perhaps, or Ambrose] had not brought them to the fore by teaching me about them.'

Augustine is here speaking out of experience. And it is that experience of a man's quest and discovery which some-how reverberates in the lives of others and is called prayer. When Ferdinand Ebner says that 'to speak of God except in a context of prayer is to take his name in vain' it means that to speak of him without yourself being in relationship with him, without seeking and finding again and again, is to talk vapouring nonsense. To speak of him at all adequately we must use personal language: it can be so personal in fact that its only parallel is in human loving and the language of the heart. So I shall talk about prayer under such headings as recognition, as resistance and submission, as community. None of these things happens in mid-air. They are all func-tions of being engaged with someone. The totality of it can only be put in the name of that someone. For a lover it is the name of the one he loves. This is delicately expressed in a poem from Paul Verlaine's *La Bonne Chanson* in which he assembles the things which the name of his beloved bring to mind:

> Une sainte en son auréole
> Une châtelaine en sa tour
> Tout ce que contient la parole
> Humaine de grace et d'amour
>
> (A saint in her circle of light
> A princess in her tower
> All that human speech contains
> Of grace and of love)

More images and recollections follow, and it ends

> Je vois, j'entends toutes ces choses
> Dans son nom Carlovingien
>
> (I see, I hear all these things
> In her name Carlovingien)

For the person at prayer it is the mysterious name of God, calling up memories, recognising a presence and opening up hope.

> . . . Lovers don't see their embraces
> as a viable theme for debate, nor a monk his prayers
>   (do they, in fact, remember them?): O's of passion,
> interior acts of attention, not being a story
>   in which the names don't matter but the way of telling[1]

Certainly this is not a story where the name doesn't matter. Cast your mind back to Mark Santer's lecture. The name matters entirely. Its content can only be known from the inside. And the Christian tradition, being at heart a tradition of prayer and worship, the story of a loving, can only be understood by those who join in and do it. This leads into a

[1] W. H. Auden's poem 'The Cave of Nakedness', in *About the House*, Faber.

consideration of prayer as recognition, and in particular the mutual recognition of individual and tradition.

Anyone who prays is at once doing something very traditional and very personal. At once he takes seriously himself as he is today, and also truths and images much older than that, hidden away in the recesses. He finds that the old images and truths evoke and clarify what he is today when 'some other person' (Jesus, Jeremiah, Augustine, Bonhoeffer or whoever) brings them to the fore by teaching him about them: it is not unknown for someone to find that the words of a service used day after day are the very words he is wanting to speak at present. It is the day's experience which gives urgent content to saying 'O God make speed to save us', or 'O Lord make clean our hearts within us.' What happens to us convinces us that these are things we want. And so, going the other way about, a man praying finds that present experience evokes and clarifies the truth of the tradition.

Prayer, by joining the personal and the traditional, is a moment of recognition. By that I mean the one thing that makes us happy above everything else, for recognition is what we all long for. The simplest example is when somebody, loaded with perplexities and half-grasped ideas, is talking to someone else, and that someone else, after listening, says something which gathers it all up, focuses it, and so opens a way forward. What is said may be something as banal and traditional as 'Where there's a will there's a way' or 'God loves you', but it is felt as new and helpful. A more far-reaching example is when somebody recognises you for what you are, knows you, to use Biblical language, and accepts that. That is recognition under its highest form of love, and it is what enables us to go on living. We would not have known what we were, let alone dared to be it, if someone else had not brought it to the fore by teaching us about it, and this is what the language and images of tradition can do for us.

To see it in the context of prayer we can go to Thomas Traherne who, with an instinct commoner than we might believe, saw 'Evry Thing being Sublimely Rich & Great & Glorious. Evry Spire of Grass is the Work of His Hand: And I in a World where evry Thing is mine, & far better than the Greater sort of Children esteem Diamonds & Pearls.' But 'I was so Ignorant that I did not think any Man in the World had had such thoughts before. Seeing them therefore so Amiable, I wondered not a little, that nothing was Spoken of them in former Ages: but as I read the Bible I was here & there Surprized with such Thoughts, & found by Degrees that these Things had been written of before, not only in the Scriptures but in many of the Fathers & that this was the Way of Communion with God in all Saints, as I saw clearly in the Person of David. Me thoughts a New Light Darted into all his Psalmes, and finally spread abroad over the whole Bible. So that things, which for their Obscurity I thought not in being, were contained: Things which for their Greatness were incredible, were made Evident & Things Obscure, Plain. GOD by this means bringing me into the very Heart of His Kingdom.' So tradition gave Traherne the courage of his convictions, and his convictions gave life to tradition. So a solitary experience became a 'Communion with God in all Saints' in a moment of recognition. In a similar way Luther found himself and more in a study of the Psalms, with consequences far beyond

his life and time: 'wherefore, whoever wants to understand
the scriptures wisely needs to understand all these things
tropologically: truth, wisdom, salvation, justice namely
with which he makes us strong, saved, just, wise'. 'From
this point', he wrote later, 'the whole face of the scriptures
was altered.'

So prayer holds the happiness of the moment of recognition—the moment of mutuality—'this is for me'. In the
words of Adam, when the Lord introduced him to Eve,
'This at last is bone of my bones and flesh of my flesh.' It is
the prodigal son 'Through seas of shipwreck home at last'.
So, when George Herbert writes his poem 'Prayer' he caps
a dazzling collection of images and descriptions with the
plain final words, 'something understood'.

> Prayer the Churches banquet, Angels age,
>   God's breath in man returning to his birth,
>   The soul in paraphrase, heart in pilgrimage,
> The Christian plummet sounding heav'n and earth:
>
> Engine against th'Almightie, sinner's towre,
>   Reversèd thunder, Christ-side-piercing spear,
>   The six daies-world transposing in an houre,
> A kind of tune, which all things heare and fear;
>
> Softnesse, and peace, and joy, and love, and blisse,
>   Exalted manna, gladnesse of the best,
>   Heaven in ordinarie, man well drest,
> The milkie way, the bird of paradise,
>   Church-bels beyond the starres heard, the souls
>   bloud,
>   The land of spices; something understood.

But an essential warning must be given here against too quick and easy an arriving at these moments. Readers of Herbert will be aware of the testing and judgment he had to go through, the impatience, reluctance and darkness he explored and expressed as well as the sweetness and light of his homecomings.

It is a temptation which everyone knows, to trick himself out in virtues and insights which do not really belong to him. To succumb to it is to lose before we start because we deny the validity of the today where we are. The word of God addresses a man where he is, so he gains nothing by being somewhere else, even in wish and imagination. Last term an anonymous master of the spiritual life wrote in yellow chalk on the Pitt Press Building 'Today is the first day of the rest of your life.' If we take up false attitudes today we cannot hope for genuine moments of recognition tomorrow. It may sound banal, but to avoid being someone else, to avoid being elsewhere, requires a determined act of resistance. You get the flavour of this in the studied ambiguity of the attitude to 'the world' in St John's gospel, or, for that matter, in a contrast of the first two chapters of St Paul's letter to the Romans with the eighth. God loves the world, and this is evident because in Christ he is both present in it, and working out its salvation to a fuller life. It is evident in the insistence on the flesh and body of Jesus. But also God, in Christ, is against the world. It is resisted and overcome, not out of mere bloody-mindedness, but in order that it may receive a peace and a kingdom which are not its own. And this is evident in the insistence on judgment, spirit as against flesh, and the second birth.

There is a parable of it in the working of any creative

artist, thinker, scientist or lover. These people are *contra mundum*. They separate themselves from ordinary distraction, sometimes to the point of eccentricity. Called absent-minded, they are in fact present-minded, because they do this in order to be present with some particular point of the world—to love it and know it—the artist and lover with a particular face, for instance, the scientist with a particular cell or organism. The resistance is in the service of knowing and recognising.

Prayer because it is recognition is also such an aggressive act. If I understand R. D. Laing correctly he has something to say to us here. His *Politics of Experience*[1] amounts to a defence of the validity of the individual's internal experience against external pressure—'the alienated starting point of our pseudo-sanity'. He pins his faith on a man like his patient Jesse Watkins going on his journey into the interior: 'Yes, the—that was the enormity of it, that I—that there was no way of avoiding this—facing up to what I—the journey I had to do.' The journey meant taking on the 'enormity of knowing', and ended in a return to a world where 'the grass was greener, the sun was shining brighter, and people were more alive, I could see them clearer'. For each of us there is a journey and, like the Jumblies, we must heed not what men say but take it:

> They went to sea in a sieve they did
>   In a sieve they went to sea:
> In spite of all their friends could say
> On a winter's morn, on a stormy day,
>   In a sieve they went to sea!

[1] Penguin Book.

> And everyone said, who saw them go,
> 'O won't they be soon upset you know!
> For the sky is dark, and the voyage is long,
> And, happen what may, it's extremely wrong,
> In a sieve to sail so fast!'

For here is the possibility, and indeed the promise, of finding 'a land all covered with trees', furnished with delightful and useful commodities, and of returning mysteriously taller. I can do no better here than to quote from Alan Ecclestone's pamphlet *On Praying*: 'The kind of resistance with which our praying is concerned includes both the willingness to tackle seemingly intractable experience and the patient maintenance and defence of the positions we have already taken up. Such prayer includes the vigilance and the audacity necessary to keep alive spiritually in circumstances which always threaten to choke and smother us. "Our fidelities", Péguy wrote, "are citadels: they do in the long run make, constitute, raise a monument to the face of God." '[1] The man who prays has to go into his room and shut the door, both to be with his Father who is in secret and to exclude the insistent voices of fashionable witch-doctors, his own distractions, and not least the admonitions of anxious orthodoxy. The courage to do this can only come from the assurance that he matters as he is, and this assurance is itself a gift of God in prayer, something he must always ask for and receive.

Here, in resisting instant orthodoxy, tradition comes to our aid—surprisingly perhaps. It might be the story of Jacob's wrestling which gives a frame and a validity to what

[1] Prism Publications.

someone is going through. Jacob, left alone at the ford Jabbok at night, wrestles with a mysterious man who puts his thigh out of joint. Then he said, 'Let me go for the day is breaking.' But Jacob said, 'I will not let you go unless you bless me.' So in the end the wounded patriarch limps off into the dawn with a blessing and a new name: 'Israel, for you have striven with God and with men and have prevailed', and a pain in the leg to remind him of it. A new name and a new reality. Or one may take the story of Job, his refusal to be deflected by the well-meaning advice of pious friends. It is to him that God in the end reveals himself:

'I had heard of thee by the hearing of the ear,
   but now my eye sees thee,
Therefore I despise myself
   and repent in dust and ashes.'

As for the friends, God is angry with them 'for you have not spoken of me what is right, as my servant Job has'. The hope for them is that 'my servant Job shall pray for you, and I will accept his prayer not to deal with you according to your folly'.

In our own time we have a powerful example of this in Britten's *War Requiem*, where the traditional Latin Mass for the dead runs alongside Wilfred Owen's passionate war poems. Sometimes the two are in flat contradiction, sometimes in a sort of agreement; but at others, as in the *Agnus Dei* coupled with Owen's 'One ever hangs where shell'd roads part', they are wonderfully together. These moments of coincidence and, very precisely, compassion, are all the more moving for not having been reached easily. I suggest that we have here a paradigm of the Christian's living with tradition.

The point of all this is summarised in words of Teilhard de Chardin: 'Unless I do everything I can to advance or resist, I shall not find myself at the required point—I shall not submit to God as much as I might have done or as much as he wishes. If, on the contrary, I persevere courageously, I shall rejoin God across evil, deeper down than evil.'[1] But notice what is going on here. In both these Old Testament stories we see the solitary wrestling of a man with the divine. His prayer is an 'engine against th'Almightie'. But the issue of it is not solitary. Jacob is given a name which is to become the name of a people. Job is declared to be the one who can offer sacrifice for others. The particular point of the lonely struggle becomes the gathering point of community. The isolation and anguish of the cross becomes, according to St John, the place of the gathering together in unity of the scattered children of God. Just as Traherne's experience of the glorious world, focused in scripture, became a communion with God in all saints, so this other dark individual experience is also a communion with others. We are dealing here with a familiar Biblical pattern, the clustering of all human need and hope round one event as creatures of the night gather around a solitary light. As it says in the Christmas hymn:

> The hopes and fears of all the years
> Are met in thee tonight.

This too, is something which happens when a man is praying. He becomes such a meeting point even in his solitude. I will try to give some description of this.

[1] *Le Milieu Divin*, Collins.

In his Hulsean Lectures, *Prayer and Providence*, Peter Baelz told us that 'Prayer is for the particular, but it deals with things in the spirit of the artist and the discoverer, and not that of the manufacturer.' The particular dealt with in the spirit of the artist and the discoverer—this is what I shall try to look at. Having glimpsed some discoverers, the Jumblies, let us turn to some artists.

Some time before he was executed for losing a battle in AD 303 the Chinese poet Lu Chi wrote an extended meditation on the poet's art. This, in the discreet rhetoric of his time, is something of what he says about the poet:

> Taking his position at the hub of things he contemplates
> the mystery of the universe;
> He feeds his emotions and his mind on the great works of
> the past. Moving along with the four seasons, he sighs
> at the passing of time;
> Gazing at the myriad objects, he thinks of the complexity
> of the world.

There is a sense, which Traherne knew well, in which each of us is at the hub of things. The world is made for us and we for the world. That is something we can take seriously. But more than that, for the poet this is a position which he takes explicitly and for a purpose, a centre of receptivity. The man of prayer, with his daily discipline, is equally explicit and deliberate. We do it to 'take upon us the mystery of things/As if we were God's spies'.

Keats is saying something similar in one of his letters: 'At once it struck me what quality went to make a man of achievement especially in literature and which Shakespeare possessed so enormously—I mean negative capability, that is when a man is capable of being in uncertainties, mysteries, doubts, without any irritable reaching after fact and reason.' In those last words we catch the note of resistance again. We resist in order that we may be able to see what is going on— and then make a proper and mature submission to it. The whirligig of everyday events often means that we don't see anything at all. To pray is to take time to look, to see what's going on and let it speak to us in the way of the blind, night vision of the poet in Shakespeare's Sonnet XLIII:

> When most I wink, then do mine eyes best see
> For all the day they view things unrespected
> But when I sleep in dreams they look on thee
> And darkly bright are bright in dark directed.

Prayer is sleep, and prayer is vigilance. The praying man is a collecting point for experience, one who gives time for it to be seen for what it is. His prayer first gathers things together, with tradition perhaps upholding and giving reference to his day-by-day experience, and then holds it up in supplication, penitence, or thanksgiving to the light of God. *This is the point at which things begin to happen.* The poet's ordered and digested experience is put in poems which can make a difference to other people, comforting or surprising them. The Christian's ordered and digested experience is put in prayers which Herbert describes as working effectually in two directions; 'Engine against th'Almightie', and 'a kind of tune which all things hear and fear'. In either case, when the poet has written or a man has prayed, things cannot be quite the same again. A difference has been made at the heart of things which reverberates into other lives. 'The power of God's love', says John Burnaby, 'takes effect in human history in no other way than through the wills and actions of men in whom that love has come to dwell. To pray is to open the heart to the entry of love—to ask God in; and where God is truly wanted he will always come. What happens when I pray is, to begin with, an encroachment of the love of God upon the defences of myself, my hard heart and laggard will.'[1]

This idea, of the individual at prayer being a point at which things start to happen, enables us to say something about intercession. A man praying is, so to speak, open at both ends. We have already seen how the lonely struggles with God of Jacob, Job, and Jesus issued in a communal blessing. Their final victory-cum-submission to the divine kingdom was for the sake of other people and for their benefit. In them, both the community of human experience and the ways of God with men found a focus, so that starting from them something happens to affect men and, if I may say so, God. Certainly I can say that a revelation of the being of God takes place because of them, their steadfastness and refusal to be put off. Imagine, if you like, that they are points towards which the human and the divine gather, and also— using the same diagram—points from which the human and the divine spread out. Put in crude visual form it looks something like this:

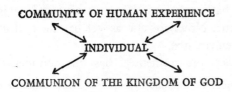

COMMUNITY OF HUMAN EXPERIENCE

INDIVIDUAL

COMMUNION OF THE KINGDOM OF GOD

[1] From *Soundings*, CUP.

H

Let us consider this double aspect of intercession a little more expansively. From the human side it is not hard to understand. If I take ten minutes every day to think about what has happened to me and about the people I have met, then all this experience, viewed unrespected in the day, finds a place where it can rest, where it is seen for what it is, where it is recognised. So W. H. Auden describes the dying Sigmund Freud:

> For about him till the very end were still
> those he had studied, the fauna of the night,
>   and shades that still waited to enter
> the bright circle of his recognition.[1]

That last line provides a description of prayer and an incentive towards it. Let us be quite clear that this recognition is doing something. It makes a difference.

About our praying for other people Ecclestone says this: 'They have needs of their own, secret needs no other person knows, but the prolonged holding of their needy condition in the attention we give is what really matters. A recognition of their need has been lodged in the fabric of our experience.'[2] And Nédoncelle: 'When I pray that enemies may be reconciled I have already, through God's action, reconciled them in myself. There is something in them that has achieved harmony, and this something only exists in and through me. Nowhere else as yet has their ultimate condition been reached.'[3]

The poet, pre-eminently, has this confidence that his

---

[1] In Memory of Sigmund Freud, from *Collected Shorter Poems 1966*, Faber.
[2] *Ibid.*   [3] *The Nature and Use of Prayer*, Burns & Oates.

experience is potentially more than individual. 'He never ceased to believe', writes Willa Muir of her husband Edwin, 'that his experience resembled the experience of everyone else involved in the process of living on earth.'[1] And the poet crystallises this in writings which will help us to see and understand a little more of the reality which we are enmeshed in, giving us the courage to be and to see a little more because what we half suspected has been held and recognised. Similarly the prayer which gathers things becomes a sprig of energy and refreshment.

From the divine side it is, of course, harder to describe. The Christian believes that when he prays the world around him does not only enter 'the bright circle of his' own 'recognition', but also and of more far reaching and mysterious consequence, the bright circle of God's recognition. He is leading things back, not just to himself as a hub of experience, but to God as the hub and source of all that is, by whose will they are and were created. This comes about in his penitence, thanksgiving, and petition, which are not just his letting himself feel these things (basic as that is) but his saying he is sorry *to God*, thanking *God*, asking *God*. God is, according to the tradition which waits to become ours, pre-eminently the place where things start to happen. The Christian knows himself as a poor man and a hungry man and his God as the one who enriches and feeds him, renewing in him the miracle of calling light out of darkness, calling into existence things which are not so that they are. It matters very much that he prays, but beside the fact that God works in his prayer that is almost inconsequential. It is the divine name that is the most real and valid thing in his

[1] *Belonging*, Hogarth Press.

praying, the name which guarantees everything about his prayer. This is the heart of it, and of this it is impossible to speak. It is not a viable theme for debate.

Having reached a point as exalted as that there is nothing to do but to climb down. The only way from the mountain of vision is down to the plains populated by ordinary human unhappiness and enjoyment. The connection between me today and the eternal God which has been made in prayer and fastened by tradition waits to be worked out in thousands of ways on the ordinary plain. I have dealt with the focus of prayer as best I can and tried to say something about what is going on when a man is consciously praying. A connection is made there of today and tradition, me and the other, the world and God. It is a spring of action running over into ordinary life. It is a moment of recognition which means that things will never look quite the same again. I have used the analogy of poetry, and in case that seems to you to be rather esoteric, something of an optional extra, may I point you to the great poetry of the Psalms? There, and especially in the psalms of lament and penitence, we find something that is both strikingly and uninhibitedly personal and at the same time traditional and generalised. Reading them we are in no doubt that a particular person is speaking from a particular point in his living. But if we ask precisely what is the matter with him (is he suffering from influenza or disappointment in love? who are the enemies he goes on about?) we are baffled. He uses, and finds it appropriate to use, the old images of the pit, the overwhelming waters, ambush and death. There is a sort of precision here, but because it is put in images rather than personal details, it is something which we can enter, a place of rest and recognition for our troubles and the troubles of those near to us. In this way the personal is not excluded but made inclusive. 'This prayer of offering', says Nédoncelle, 'consists in presenting oneself and the world to God, in such a way that the realm of created beings, in spite of everything that afflicts it, is subjected to God and becomes holy, co-operating in the movement which originates from him.'[1] In Herbert's words: 'God's breath in man returning to his birth.'

'Only connect the poetry and the prose and both will be exalted.' E. M. Forster points us on the way. We are not to be ashamed of the sublime or the ordinary, nor shirk either, nor should we be ashamed of being new or of being traditional. For this purpose we make our act of resistance, to allow the 'negative capability' of being in the presence of things as they are. We cultivate, in fact, a double confidence —in things as they are and in the vision of things as they can be in the Kingdom of God—by observing both, by holding in ourselves the tension between them. Only if we take each seriously as it is will the connection between them, the moments of recognition, be genuine. Only so can energy flow out from there to renew both the vision of God and the face of the earth.

You get this insistence in Stanley Spencer's superb assertion, 'I believe in angels and dirt.' The two do indeed belong together. You get it in the teaching of Jesus where glory and the joy of angels happen around the morally dirty publican as he repents, and not around the purer pharisee who considers himself exalted above the dirt. We think of saints as those who are on terms with the sublime. Ought we not to think of them too as those who have come to terms with the

[1] *The Nature and Use of Prayer*, Burns & Oates.

degraded and degrading? For it is there, we are told at Christmas and at Easter, that the wonderful is to be found. This is a theme of Patrick White's novel *Riders in the Chariot*. It is about four people who have seen the vision of the chariot throne attended by living creatures, and the effect which this has on the history of their lives. At the end only one is left, Mrs Godbold, going home to her shack in the evening:

'Even though it was her habit to tread straight, she would remain a plodding simpleton. From behind, her great beam, under the stretchy cardigan, might have appeared something of a joke, except to the few who happened to perceive that she also wore the crown.

That evening, as she walked along the road, it was the hour at which the other gold sank its furrows in the softer sky. The lids of her eyes, flickering beneath its glow, were gilded with an identical splendour. But for all its weight, it lay lightly upon her, in fact, to where she remained an instant in the company of the living creatures she had known, and many others she had not.

If on further visits . . . she experienced nothing comparable, it was probably because Mrs. Godbold's feet were still planted firmly on the earth. She would lower her eyes to avoid the dazzle, and walk on, breathing heavily, for it was a stiff pull up the hill, to the shed in which she continued to live.'[1]

So, for all of us, life must go on. But that is not a deprivation. If we are there, we are in the place where God can encounter us, being a God not of the dead but of the living.

[1] Penguin Books.

And it is here that we find the material of our prayer and
find what desperately needs our prayer. A sign of genuine
holiness is that it is grounded, feet planted firmly on the
earth. The incidents of the everyday world, says de Chardin,
are the rungs of the ladder where the traffic is up and down
between heaven and earth. It has been written of the poetry
of Gerard Manley Hopkins, with its close attention both to
nature and to God, 'Just as Christ is reborn to the world
through the witness of one brave martyr, so the grandeur of
God will "flame out", beautiful and awe-inspiring, from the
imperfect "perfection" of one of his creatures. Their duller
glory can be converted into a divine irradiance when such
a sight "meets" a human heart in a receptive and perceptive
mood.'[1]

But the important thing remains—whether or not you
choose to occupy yourself in praying. I have not suggested
any techniques, this not being a story in which the names
don't matter, but the way of telling. But I'll end with two
bits of advice. One is from a poem by C. Day Lewis, in
which an old priest of an unspecified religion is teaching the
trade to a novice. He says:

> But the crucial point is this:
> You are called only to make the sacrifice:
> Whether or not he enters into it
> Is the God's affair; and whatever the handbooks say
> You can neither command his presence or explain it—
> All you can do is to make it possible.
> If the sacrifice catches fire of its own accord
> On the altar, well and good. But do not

[1] N. H. Mackenzie, *Hopkins*, Oliver & Boyd.

Flatter yourself that discipline and devotion
Have wrought the miracle: they have only allowed it,[1]

The other is based on lines from T. S. Eliot's 'Little Gidding',
which take up the teaching of Julian of Norwich:

> And all shall be well and
> All manner of things shall be well
> By the purification of the motive
> In the ground of our beseeching.[2]

'We do not know how to pray as we ought', says St Paul.
It is a statement that needs no questioning. Our major task
in praying is to seek out the prayer which we should pray—
the prayer which is really ours and really God's, which is
genuinely mutual in fact. In this his presence, his spirit, helps
us by witnessing along with our spirit. From this co-
operation the word which eventually breaks out as the true
word is (surprisingly and against so much probability) the
cry of appeal and recognition 'Abba—Father'.

It matters little, with praying, where one starts or how one
starts, so long as it is one's real self that is engaged. And the
tradition—I have laboured the point—is there to help and
confirm us. What does matter is the presence which we can
neither command nor explain, that 'certain name' on which
we call. The name of God is the promise of his presence, a
presence working in the ground of the heart, sorting out and
educating the motives behind our beseeching. So if there is
one basic prayer for all of us I would say that it is the old one,
'O God make clean our hearts within us.' Ordinary ex-

[1] Final Instructions, *Selected Poems*, Penguin Books.
[2] *Four Quartets*, Faber.

perience, if we are at all thoughtful, will leave us in no doubt about the need of it, the need of a perceptive and receptive centre for all our living. And if there is one thing entirely certain about prayer it is that we will find that the age-old words 'I am the Lord thy God' are true for us in our today.